Grade 3

Pearson Scott Foresman

Leveled Reader
Teaching Guide

Glenview, Illinois • Boston, Massachusetts • Chandler, Arizona • Upper Saddle River, New Jersey

ISBN: 13: 978-0-328-48448-5
ISBN: 10:   0-328-48448-2
3 4 5 6 7 8 9 10 V031 15 14 13 12 11

Table of Contents

LEVELED READER TITLE	Instruction	Comprehension Practice	Vocabulary Practice
The Opposite Cousins	12–13	14	15
It's a Fair Swap!	16–17	18	19
Life in the Arctic	20–21	22	23
Let's Surprise Mom	24–25	26	27
E-mail Friends	28–29	30	31
The Frozen Continent: Antarctica	32–33	34	35
Buddy Goes to School	36–37	38	39
The Metal Detective	40–41	42	43
Growing Vegetables	44–45	46	47
All About Birds	48–49	50	51
Raisins	52–53	54	55
The Hunters and the Elk	56–57	58	59
Pictures in the Sky	60–61	62	63
Rescuing Whales	64–65	66	67
The Field Trip	68–69	70	71
The Winning Point!	72–73	74	75
How to Measure the Weather	76–77	78	79
Grandpa's Rock Kit	80–81	82	83

Graphic Organizers

Introduction

Scott Foresman *Reading Street* provides more than 750 leveled readers that help children become better readers and build a lifelong love of reading. The *Reading Street* leveled readers are engaging texts that help children practice critical reading skills and strategies. They also provide opportunities to build vocabulary, understand concepts, and develop reading fluency.

The leveled readers were developed to be age-appropriate and appealing to children at each grade level. The leveled readers consist of engaging texts in a variety of genres, including fantasy, folk tales, realistic fiction, historical fiction, and narrative and expository nonfiction. To better address real-life reading skills that children will encounter in testing situations and beyond, a higher percentage of nonfiction texts is provided at each grade.

USING THE LEVELED READERS

You can use the leveled readers to meet the diverse needs of your children. Consider using the readers to

- practice critical skills and strategies
- build fluency
- build vocabulary and concepts
- build background for the main selections in the student book
- provide a variety of reading experiences, e.g., shared, group, individual, take-home, readers' theater

GUIDED READING APPROACH

The *Reading Street* leveled readers are leveled according to Guided Reading criteria by experts trained in Guided Reading. The Guided Reading levels increase in difficulty within a grade level and across grade levels. In addition to leveling according to Guided Reading criteria, the instruction provided in the *Leveled Reader Teaching Guide* is compatible with Guided Reading instruction. An instructional routine is provided for each leveled reader. This routine is most effective when working with individual children or small groups.

MANAGING THE CLASSROOM

When using the leveled readers with individuals or small groups, you'll want to keep the other children engaged in meaningful, independent learning tasks. Establishing independent practice stations throughout the classroom and child routines for these stations can help you manage the rest of the class while you work with individuals or small groups. Practice stations can include listening, phonics, vocabulary, independent reading, and cross-curricular activities. For classroom management, create a work board that lists the stations and which children should be at each station. Provide instructions at each station that detail the tasks to be accomplished. Update the board and alert children when they should rotate to a new station. For additional support for managing your classroom, see the *Reading Street* Practice Stations' *Classroom Management Handbook*.

USING THE LEVELED READER TEACHING GUIDE

The *Leveled Reader Teaching Guide* provides an instruction plan for each leveled reader based on the same instructional routine.

INTRODUCE THE BOOK The Introduction includes suggestions for creating interest in the text by discussing the title and author, building background, and previewing the book and its features.

READ THE BOOK Before students begin reading the book, have them set purposes for reading and discuss how they can use the reading strategy as they read. Determine how you want students in a particular group to read the text, softly or silently, to a specific point or the entire text. Then use the Comprehension Questions to provide support as needed and to assess comprehension.

REVISIT THE BOOK The Reader Response questions provide opportunities for students to demonstrate their understanding of the text, the target comprehension skill, and vocabulary. The Response Options require students to revisit the text to respond to what they've read and to move beyond the text to explore related content.

SKILL WORK The Skill Work box provides instruction and practice for the target skill and strategy and selection vocabulary. Instruction for an alternate comprehension skill allows teachers to provide additional skill instruction and practice for students.

USING THE GRAPHIC ORGANIZERS

Graphic organizers in blackline-master format can be found on pages 132–152. These can be used as overhead transparencies or as student worksheets.

ASSESSING PERFORMANCE

Use the assessment forms that begin on page 6 to make notes about your students' reading skills, use of reading strategies, and general reading behaviors.

MEASURE FLUENT READING (pp. 6–7) Provides directions for measuring a student's fluency, based on words correct per minute (wcpm), and reading accuracy using a running record.

OBSERVATION CHECKLIST (p. 8) Allows you to note the regularity with which students demonstrate their understanding and use of reading skills and strategies.

STUDENT SELF-ASSESSMENT (p. 9) Helps students identify their own areas of strength and areas where they need further work. This form (About My Reading) encourages them to list steps they can take to become better readers and to set goals as readers. Suggest that students share their self-assessment notes with their families so that family members can work with them more effectively to practice their reading skills and strategies at home.

READING STRATEGY ASSESSMENT (p. 10) Provides criteria for evaluating each student's proficiency as a strategic reader.

PROGRESS REPORT (p. 11) Provides a means to track a student's book-reading progress over a period of time by noting the level at which a student reads and his or her accuracy at that level. Reading the chart from left to right gives you a visual model of how quickly a student is making the transition from one level to the next. Share these reports with parents or guardians to help them see how their child's reading is progressing.

Measure
Fluent Reading

Taking a Running Record

A running record is an assessment of a student's oral reading accuracy and oral reading fluency. Reading accuracy is based on the number of words read correctly. Reading fluency is based on the reading rate (the number of words correct per minute) and the degree to which a student reads with a "natural flow."

How to Measure Reading Accuracy

1. Choose a grade-level text of about 80 to 120 words that is unfamiliar to the student.
2. Make a copy of the text for yourself. Make a copy for the student or have the student read aloud from a book.
3. Give the student the text and have the student read aloud. (You may wish to record the student's reading for later evaluation.)
4. On your copy of the text, mark any miscues or errors the student makes while reading. See the running record sample on page 7, which shows how to identify and mark miscues.
5. Count the total number of words in the text and the total number of errors made by the student. Note: If a student makes the same error more than once, such as mispronouncing the same word multiple times, count it as one error. Self-corrections do not count as actual errors. Use the following formula to calculate the percentage score, or accuracy rate:

$$\frac{\text{Total Number of Words} - \text{Total Number of Errors}}{\text{Total Number of Words}} \times 100 = \text{percentage score}$$

Interpreting the Results

- A student who reads **95–100%** of the words correctly is reading at an **independent level** and may need more challenging text.
- A student who reads **90–94%** of the words correctly is reading at an **instructional level** and will likely benefit from guided instruction.
- A student who reads **89%** or fewer of the words correctly is reading at a **frustrational level** and may benefit most from targeted instruction with lower-level texts and intervention.

How to Measure Reading Rate (WCPM)

1. Follow Steps 1–3 above.
2. Note the exact times when the student begins and finishes reading.
3. Use the following formula to calculate the number of words correct per minute (WCPM):

$$\frac{\text{Total Number of Words Read Correctly}}{\text{Total Number of Seconds}} \times 60 = \text{words correct per minute}$$

Interpreting the Results

By the end of the year, a third-grader should be reading approximately 110–120 WCPM.

Running Record Sample

Running Record Sample

Dana had recently begun ✓✓✓✓✓ **4**

volunteering at the animal rescue ✓✓✓✓✓ **9**

shelter where her mom worked as a ✓✓✓✓✓✓✓ **16**

veterinarian. The shelter was (just) across ✓✓✓✓ **22**

the bay from their house. ✓✓✓✓✓ **27**

Dana was learning many different ✓✓✓✓✓ H **32**

jobs at the shelter. She fed the dogs ✓✓✓✓✓✓ **40**

and cleaned their cages. She played ✓✓✓✓✓ **46**

catch with the dogs in the shelter's ✓✓✓✓✓✓ **53**

backyard. Dana's favorite job, however, ✓✓✓ /jōb/ ✓ **58**

was introducing people to the dogs ✓✓✓✓✓ **64**

waiting for adoption. Whenever a dog ✓✓✓✓✓✓ **70**

found a new home, Dana was (sc) especially ✓✓✓✓✓ **77**

pleased! ✓ **78**

The road to the shelter crossed over ✓✓✓✓✓✓✓ **85**

the bay. Dana looked for boats in the ✓✓✓✓ the ✓✓✓ **93**

channel, but there were none. Dana's ✓✓✓✓^✓ **99**

mom turned on the radio to listen to ✓✓✓✓✓ hear **107**

the news as they drove. The weather ✓✓✓✓✓✓ **114**

reporter announced that a blizzard ✓✓✓✓ **119**

might hit some parts of the state. ✓✓✓✓✓✓ **126**

Notations

Accurate Reading
The student reads a word correctly.

Omission
The student omits words or word parts.

Hesitation
The student hesitates over a word, and the teacher provides the word. Wait several seconds before telling the student what the word is.

Mispronunciation/Misreading
The student pronounces or reads a word incorrectly.

Self-correction
The student reads a word incorrectly but then corrects the error. Do not count self-corrections as actual errors. However, noting self-corrections will help you identify words the student finds difficult.

Insertion
The student inserts words or parts of words that are not in the text.

Substitution
The student substitutes words or parts of words for the words in the text.

Running Record Results
Total Number of Words: **126**
Number of Errors: **5**

Reading Time: **64 seconds**

▶ **Reading Accuracy**
$$\frac{126 - 5}{126} \times 100 = 96.032 = 96\%$$

Accuracy Percentage Score: **96%**

▶ **Reading Rate—WCPM**
$$\frac{121}{64} \times 60 = 113.44 = 113 \text{ words correct per minute}$$

Reading Rate: **113 WCPM**

Observation Checklist

Student's Name _____ Date _____

Behaviors Observed	Always (Proficient)	Usually (Fluent)	Sometimes (Developing)	Rarely (Novice)
Reading Strategies and Skills				
Uses prior knowledge and preview to understand what book is about				
Makes predictions and checks them while reading				
Uses context clues to figure out meanings of new words				
Uses phonics and syllabication to decode words				
Self-corrects while reading				
Reads at an appropriate reading rate				
Reads with appropriate intonation and stress				
Uses fix-up strategies				
Identifies story elements: character, setting, plot, theme				
Summarizes plot or main ideas accurately				
Uses target comprehension skill to understand the text better				
Responds thoughtfully about the text				
Reading Behaviors and Attitudes				
Enjoys listening to stories				
Chooses reading as a free-time activity				
Reads with sustained interest and attention				
Participates in discussion about books				

General Comments

About My Reading

Name _____ Date _____

1. **Compared with earlier in the year, I am enjoying reading**

   ☐ more   ☐ less   ☐ about the same

2. **When I read now, I understand**

   ☐ more than I used to   ☐ about the same as I used to

3. **One thing that has helped me with my reading is**

   _____

   _____

   _____

4. **One thing that could make me a better reader is**

   _____

   _____

   _____

5. **Here is one selection or book that I really enjoyed reading:**

   _____

   _____

6. **Here are some reasons why I liked it:**

   _____

   _____

   _____

   _____

   _____

   _____

Reading Strategy Assessment ✓

Student _____ Date _____

Teacher _____

		Proficient	Developing	Emerging	Not showing trait
Building Background Comments:	Previews	☐	☐	☐	☐
	Asks questions	☐	☐	☐	☐
	Predicts	☐	☐	☐	☐
	Activates prior knowledge	☐	☐	☐	☐
	Sets own purposes for reading	☐	☐	☐	☐
	Other:	☐	☐	☐	☐
Comprehension Comments:	Retells/summarizes	☐	☐	☐	☐
	Questions, evaluates ideas	☐	☐	☐	☐
	Relates to self/other texts	☐	☐	☐	☐
	Paraphrases	☐	☐	☐	☐
	Rereads/reads ahead for meaning	☐	☐	☐	☐
	Visualizes	☐	☐	☐	☐
	Uses decoding strategies	☐	☐	☐	☐
	Uses vocabulary strategies	☐	☐	☐	☐
	Understands key ideas of a text	☐	☐	☐	☐
	Other:	☐	☐	☐	☐
Fluency Comments:	Adjusts reading rate	☐	☐	☐	☐
	Reads for accuracy	☐	☐	☐	☐
	Uses expression	☐	☐	☐	☐
	Other:	☐	☐	☐	☐
Connections Comments:	Relates text to self	☐	☐	☐	☐
	Relates text to text	☐	☐	☐	☐
	Relates text to world	☐	☐	☐	☐
	Other:	☐	☐	☐	☐
Self-Assessment Comments:	Is aware of: Strengths	☐	☐	☐	☐
	Needs	☐	☐	☐	☐
	Improvement/achievement	☐	☐	☐	☐
	Sets and implements learning goals	☐	☐	☐	☐
	Maintains logs, records, portfolio	☐	☐	☐	☐
	Works with others	☐	☐	☐	☐
	Shares ideas and materials	☐	☐	☐	☐
	Other:	☐	☐	☐	☐

Progress Report

Student's Name_____

At the top of the chart, record the book title, its grade/unit/week (for example, 1.2.3), and the student's accuracy percentage. See page 6 for measuring fluency, calculating accuracy and reading rates. At the bottom of the chart, record the date you took the running record. In the middle of the chart, make an X in the box across from the level of the student's reading—frustrational level (below 89% accuracy), instructional level (90–94% accuracy), or independent level (95–100% accuracy). Record the reading rate (WCPM) in the next row.

Book Title						
Grade/Unit/Week						
Reading Accuracy Percentage						
LEVEL **Frustrational** (89% or below)						
Instructional (90–94%)						
Independent (95% or above)						
Reading Rate (WCPM)						
Date						

The Opposite Cousins

SUMMARY A girl named Samantha is excited that her cousin Jeff will be spending a week at the lake with her family. Although they once had very similar interests, Samantha soon realizes that they are now very different.

LESSON VOCABULARY

bat	battery
blew	fuel
plug	term
vision	

INTRODUCE THE BOOK

INTRODUCE THE TITLE AND AUTHOR Discuss with students the title and the author of *The Opposite Cousins*. Based on the title and cover art, ask students to describe what they think this book is about.

BUILD BACKGROUND Ask students if they have a family member such as a cousin or even a friend they like to do things with. Discuss with students what they like to do with this person. Continue the discussion by asking students whether they sometimes like to do things that the other person is not interested in doing.

PREVIEW/USE ILLUSTRATIONS Have students skim through the book, looking at the pictures. Ask: What do you think the story is about? Who are the characters? Where does the story appear to take place?

ELL Ask students if they have traveled to a different city or country with a family member. Have students tell about their trips and point to their destinations on a map.

READ THE BOOK

SET PURPOSE Have students set a purpose for reading *The Opposite Cousins*. This purpose should be guided by the impressions they get from reading the title and skimming the illustrations along with their own curiosity.

STRATEGY SUPPORT: PRIOR KNOWLEDGE Remind students that *prior knowledge* is what they already know about a subject. Prior knowledge might be gathered from their reading or personal experiences. Explain that connecting prior knowledge to text can help students understand what they read. Invite students to discuss different activities they have done when visiting relatives or when on vacation.

COMPREHENSION QUESTIONS

PAGE 5 What kinds of activities does Samantha like to do while at the lake? What does Jeff do? *(Samantha likes to fish, hike, and swim. Jeff likes to play on his computer.)*

PAGE 6 What do Samantha and Jeff do on the third day when it rains? *(They play a computer game together.)*

PAGE 8 What do you think might have happened if Jeff's computer had not been damaged by the storm? *(Possible response: He may not have gone fishing with Samantha but instead stayed inside to play on his computer.)*

PAGE 11 What do you think that Samantha and Jeff might do the next time they see each other? *(Possible responses: They might work on creating the fishing computer game. They might go fishing.)*

REVISIT THE BOOK

READER RESPONSE

1. Possible responses: fish, hike, swim, spend time with Mom and Dad.
2. Responses will vary based on what students have read and experienced.
3. The author meant a flying mammal. Possible responses: a wooden or metal club; to hit. Pictures should depict the correct definitions.
4. Responses will vary but should reflect the characteristics of Samantha and Jeff.

EXTEND UNDERSTANDING Discuss with students that *plot* refers to the events in the story that carry the story from beginning to middle to end. Point out that Jeff acts differently toward Samantha in the beginning of the story compared with the end of the story. Discuss with students how Jeff acts differently in the two parts of the story.

RESPONSE OPTIONS

WRITING Ask students to imagine that they are on vacation at a lake. Have them write a letter to a friend at home describing their experiences.

WORD WORK Challenge students to write or verbalize sentences that incorporate two or more vocabulary words. Provide an example, such as, *When the battery no longer worked in the computer, I had to plug it in to give it power.*

SCIENCE CONNECTION

TIME FOR Science

Provide appropriate nonfiction books about fish, and invite students to use reference sources to learn more about different types of fish and the bodies of water where they can find fish. Have them share what they learn with the class.

Skill Work

TEACH/REVIEW VOCABULARY

Read the vocabulary words. Ask students about words they may already know. Discuss how they first heard of the words and what they think the words mean. Tell them that they will become more familiar with these words as they read.

TARGET SKILL AND STRATEGY

CHARACTER AND SETTING Tell students that a *character* is a person who takes part in the events of a story. Ask them to identify the two main characters in the book. Then explain that the qualities or characteristics of a character are known as *character traits* and that they usually relate to the character's personality. While students are reading, have them identify the character traits of Samantha and Jeff based on clues and details in the story. Additionally, remind students that the *setting* is where the story takes place. Ask children how the story might be different if it took place in a setting other than at the lake.

PRIOR KNOWLEDGE Tell students that *prior knowledge* is what they know about a given topic. Prior knowledge might be gathered from their reading and personal experiences. Explain that connecting prior knowledge to text can help students understand what they read. Read aloud sections of the book and pause to ask students what it reminds them of. Tell them to think of their own lives; previously read books; and people, places, and things in the world.

ADDITIONAL SKILL INSTRUCTION

DRAW CONCLUSIONS When students draw conclusions, they should use what they read and what they already know to figure out more than what is presented in the book. Use graphic organizers to model how to draw conclusions—a chart with columns for facts from the book, what I already know, and the conclusions that result. Have students share facts and prior knowledge while drawing conclusions about what they read in the book.

Name _____

Character and Setting

- A **character** in a story is a person or animal in a story.
- The **setting** is the time and place of a story.

Directions Complete the chart. Write details from the story that tell about the main characters, Samantha and Jeff, and the setting.

The Opposite Cousins	
Characters	**Setting**

Directions Write a paragraph explaining how the setting affects Samantha's and Jeff's actions and behaviors.

_____

_____

_____

_____

_____

_____

_____

_____

Vocabulary

Directions Choose the word from the box that best matches each definition. Write the word on the line.

Check the Words You Know

___ bat	___ battery	___ blew	___ fuel
___ plug	___ term	___ vision	

1. _____ something that is burned for power or heat

2. _____ a flying mammal

3. _____ used to produce electric energy

4. _____ connect to give power

5. _____ moved rapidly

6. _____ a period of time

7. _____ an imagined idea or plan

Directions Select three vocabulary words and write a sentence using each one.

8. _____

_____

9. _____

_____

10. _____

_____

It's A Fair Swap!

SUMMARY This nonfiction book describes bartering in early America and how, as the country grew, bartering gave way to the use of paper money.

LESSON VOCABULARY

carpenter	carpetmaker
knowledge	marketplace
merchant	plenty
straying	thread

INTRODUCE THE BOOK

INTRODUCE THE TITLE AND AUTHOR Introduce students to the title and the author of the book *It's A Fair Swap!* Based on the title, ask students what kind of information they think this book will provide. Ask students what they think the people in the cover illustration are doing and why they are doing it.

BUILD BACKGROUND Invite students to consider how they would get the things they wanted or needed if there was no money in the world. Ask students if they have ever traded or swapped something for something else. Tell students that this is called *bartering,* an act they will read and learn about in the book.

PREVIEW/USE TEXT FEATURES Invite students to take a picture walk through the illustrations. Ask students how the illustrations give clues to what the book might be about. Direct students' attention to page 12 and the thought balloon drawn over the girl's head. Ask: What do you think is happening in this particular photograph? How might it relate to the topic of the book?

READ THE BOOK

SET PURPOSE Have students set a purpose for reading *It's A Fair Swap!* Students' curiosity about swapping and bartering should guide this purpose. Suggest that students think about the necessity for bartering as they read the book.

STRATEGY SUPPORT: SUMMARIZE As students read the book, suggest that they write down and number the major ideas and milestones. After reading, have students write summary paragraphs using their notes as guides.

COMPREHENSION QUESTIONS

PAGE 4 What is the sequence of events in a barter? (*People decide what they want to trade, approach another person and determine if the goods have equal value, and either make the trade or not.*)

PAGE 4 In bartering, what must both people agree on? (*People must agree that their goods have equal value.*)

PAGE 5 Why didn't the colonists use European money in America? (*There were no stores or banks.*)

PAGE 9 Why did the farmers need to grow extra crops? (*Farmers used these extra crops to barter for things they couldn't make or grow.*)

PAGE 10 Why did the colonists start using paper money? (*It was easier to carry than crops or livestock.*)

PAGE 12 Why do you think bartering still goes on today? (*Possible responses: people do not always have money; bartering is fun.*)

REVISIT THE BOOK

READER RESPONSE

1. Correct sequence: Colonists plant or hunt their own food; the barter system is used at the general store; people begin using money to buy things from their local merchants; shopping malls replace the general stores.
2. The general store was important because it sold or bartered everything that couldn't be grown or made on a farm.
3. *know*; possible response: I know that Boston is the capital of Massachusetts.
4. Possible responses: candles, paper, books

EXTEND UNDERSTANDING Remind students that the *setting* is where and when a story takes place. Discuss with students the settings covered in pages 4–19 of *It's A Fair Swap!* Ask: Why were these particular settings conducive to bartering? Is bartering as necessary in a modern city as it was in the colonial period? Why or why not?

RESPONSE OPTIONS

WRITING Remind students that in bartering, the more valuable an item you have to trade, the more valuable an item you are likely to get in return. With this in mind, ask students to write a script for a commercial for an item they want to barter. Suggest that they use persuasive language. Ask volunteers to present their commercials to the class.

SOCIAL STUDIES CONNECTION

Time For SOCIAL STUDIES

Hand out large sheets of paper and have students divide them in half. On the left side of their papers, students should draw or paste pictures of something they want to barter. On the right side, have students draw or paste pictures of items they think might be of equal value.

Skill Work

TEACH/REVIEW VOCABULARY

After reviewing the vocabulary words with students, play Vocabulary Master. Give students a list of definitions and have them match each definition to the appropriate vocabulary word. Then have students use each word in a sentence.

ELL Write *marketplace* on the board and have students identify the two words that form this compound. Discuss how you can arrive at a definition for *marketplace* by combining the meanings of *market* and *place*. Finally have students contribute other words they know that are formed with *place* (*someplace, misplace, birthplace,* etc.).

TARGET SKILL AND STRATEGY

SEQUENCE Remind students that the *sequence* is the order in which events happen. Ask students to tell the sequence of events of getting to school each morning or of doing their homework. To further illustrate the concept, have students number each event so they can see the sequence of events more easily.

SUMMARIZE Remind students that *summarizing* is reducing what you have read into the most important ideas. It can help you understand the main points of a story. Ask students to summarize a familiar story like *The Three Bears*.

ADDITIONAL SKILL INSTRUCTION

FACT AND OPINION Remind students that a *statement of fact* is a statement which can be proved true or false and a *statement of opinion* is a belief that cannot be proved true or false. Invite students to tell you a few facts about school. Then ask for a few opinions. Discuss the difference.

Sequence

Sequence of events in a story is the order in which the events occur.

Directions To help you understand the sequence of events in *It's A Fair Swap!* use this flow chart. It is called a flow chart because one event "flows" into another, from first to last. Reread the story. As you read, answer the questions.

1. What happened first?

_____

_____

_____

↓

2. What happened next?

_____

_____

_____

↓

3. What happened after that?

_____

_____

_____

↓

4. What was the last thing that happened?

_____

_____

_____

Vocabulary

Directions Unscramble each vocabulary word and write the word on the line. Then fit each vocabulary word into the right sentence.

Check the Words You Know

___carpenter	___carpetmaker	___knowledge	___marketplace
___merchant	___plenty	___straying	___thread

1. racpeetnr   _____

2. gdnwoklee   _____

3. ketplmarace   _____

4. tylpen   _____

5. ingtsray   _____

6. raedth   _____

7. erpetcarkam   _____

8. chentmar   _____

9. The _____ built us a wonderful table.

10. I need to sew this button on my shirt, so please bring me a needle and

    _____.

11. That dog is not staying close to home but is _____.

12. There is lots of food, so there will be _____ to eat.

13. The _____ sells apples, oranges, and pears.

14. An encyclopedia contains lots of _____.

15. This rug needs repair, so we must call the _____.

16. The _____ sells many delicious fruits and vegetables.

Directions Write two sentences, using a vocabulary word in each.

17. _____

    _____

18. _____

    _____

Life in the Arctic

SUMMARY In this nonfiction book, students are introduced to the Inuit. The author describes how the Inuit people live and survive in the cold Arctic climate.

LESSON VOCABULARY

gear	parka
splendid	twitch
willow	yanked

INTRODUCE THE BOOK

INTRODUCE THE TITLE AND AUTHOR Discuss with students the title and author of *Life in the Arctic*. Based on the title, ask students what kind of information they think this book will provide.

BUILD BACKGROUND Point out to students that there are indeed people who live in the Arctic. Discuss with students the conditions that exist in places such as the Arctic and what it might take to live in these places.

PREVIEW/USE ILLUSTRATIONS Have students preview the book by looking at the illustrations. Be sure that students understand the view of the map on page 3. From looking at the illustrations, ask students to discuss what they might learn about the people and activities pictured.

READ THE BOOK

SET PURPOSE Have students set their own purposes for reading the book. Ask: What would you like to learn about the people of the Arctic? *(For example: Who are they? How do they survive? How are they different from others?)* Suggest that students look for information about these topics as they read.

STRATEGY SUPPORT: VISUALIZE Explain to students, *visualizing* is creating pictures in your mind about what is happening in the story. Explain that while the term seems to involve only the sense of sight, visualizing includes all the senses and allows a reader to become involved with what they are reading. Tell students as they visualize, they should imagine how things taste, feel, sound, smell, or look.

COMPREHENSION QUESTIONS

PAGE 6 Why is it important for the Inuit to prepare for winter? *(Possible response: The winter is long and cold, which makes it difficult to get food to survive.)*

PAGE 8 What is the last thing the Inuit do to prepare for winter? *(They move into a winter home that is made of wood or stone.)*

PAGES 9–11 What are some other things that the Inuit use to help them survive the winter? *(They wear parkas and boots. They use sleds and snowmobiles for transportation.)*

REVISIT THE BOOK

READER RESPONSE

1. First, an Inuit family hunts and fishes throughout the summer. Next, family members dry some food and save it for winter. Last, the family moves into a winter home made of wood or stone.
2. Responses will vary but should include a description of a visualization and how it relates to the selection.
3. sleds and snowmobiles
4. Responses will vary but should reflect an understanding of the selection.

EXTEND UNDERSTANDING Once students have read the book, discuss how the illustrations in the book helped them understand the text. Discuss whether the illustrations helped students visualize what was being discussed, even when there were no actions or descriptions.

RESPONSE OPTIONS

WRITING Pass out blank index cards and ask students to imagine that they are visiting the Arctic. Using information from the story, have students create postcards about their visit.

SOCIAL STUDIES CONNECTION

Time For
SOCIAL
STUDIES

Invite students to learn more about people who live in other cold climates. They could learn about the scientists who live in Antarctica or the Yup´ik from Alaska. They can use books or the Internet. Afterwards, have students share their information with each other.

ELL Ask students if they have visited or lived in a different climate and how it was different. Have them tell how people who live there dress or do things differently.

Skill Work

TEACH/REVIEW VOCABULARY

Have small groups use dictionaries to define the vocabulary words and identify their parts of speech. Then have these groups create as many categories as possible into which they can sort the words (for example, *Nouns, Past Tense Verbs, Items You Can Wear*). Ask groups to share the definitions and categories with the class.

TARGET SKILL AND STRATEGY

SEQUENCE Review with students that *sequence* is the order in which events happen. Remind students that sometimes an author uses clue words such as *first, next, then,* and *last* to show sequence. Have students look for sequence clue words as they read.

VISUALIZE Remind students that authors use descriptive words to help readers *visualize* a story. These words may tell what something looks or feels like or how it sounds, tastes, or smells. Tell students: As you read, form pictures in your mind about what is happening in the story.

ADDITIONAL SKILL INSTRUCTION

GENERALIZE Explain to students that when they read, they sometimes can make a *generalization* about several things or people as a group. A generalization statement may be about how the ideas are mostly alike or all alike. As an example, tell students that you can make a statement about how all birds are alike by saying, "All birds have feathers." As they read, have students think of a generalization statement that shows how the people of the Arctic are similar to other people around the world.

Name _____

Sequence

- **Sequence** is the order in which things happen in a story or selection—what happens first, next, and last.

Directions Read the following passage about the Inuit people. The statements are not in the right order. Write the statements in the correct sequence in the graphic organizer below.

Then, as the Inuit were able to domesticate dogs, they developed the dog sled. As technology developed even further, the Inuit began to rely on snowmobiles to carry goods. The Inuit, like many other ancient people, invented or developed new technology to help make life easier. At first, early Inuit hunters used small sleds, pulled by the hunters themselves, to transport game after a hunt.

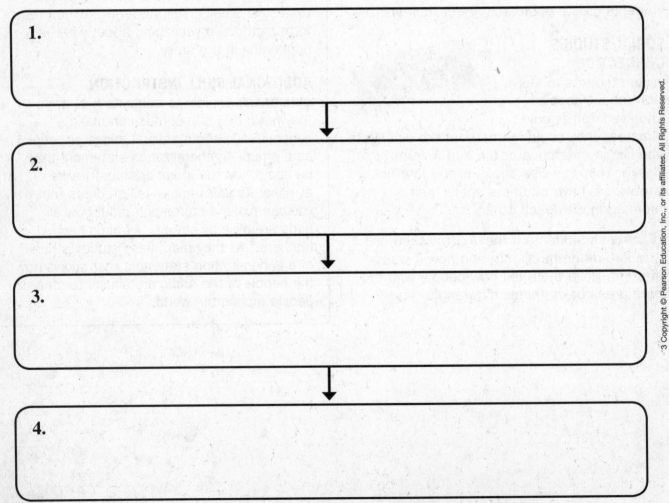

1.

2.

3.

4.

Vocabulary

Directions Draw a line from each word to its definition.

Check the Words You Know

___ gear	___ parka	___ splendid
___ twitch	___ willow	___ yanked

1. willow

2. gear

3. yanked

4. parka

5. splendid

6. twitch

a. equipment needed for a purpose

b. excellent

c. to move with a quick motion

d. a kind of tree with narrow branches

e. jerked or pulled with force

f. a heavy, fur-lined coat

Directions Use the words *gear*, *yanked*, *splendid*, and *parka* in a paragraph about winter.

_____

_____

_____

_____

_____

_____

_____

_____

_____

_____

Let's Suprise Mom

SUMMARY A boy, James, decides to surprise Mom because she is always doing nice things for him. So James and his grandmother go shopping for the ingredients to make Mom great pancakes.

LESSON VOCABULARY

laundry	section
shelves	spoiled
store	thousands
traded	variety

INTRODUCE THE BOOK

INTRODUCE THE TITLE AND AUTHOR Discuss with students the title and the author of *Let's Surprise Mom*. Based on the title and cover art, ask students to describe what they think this book is about.

BUILD BACKGROUND Ask students if they have ever baked or cooked with an adult. Discuss their experiences and whether there was a special reason for baking.

ELL Encourage students to share information about ingredients that they would use to make someone a special dish.

PREVIEW/USE ILLUSTRATIONS As students preview the book, ask them how the illustrations give them context clues to what is happening. Ask: Who are the characters in the story? Where does the story take place? What is happening in the story?

READ THE BOOK

SET PURPOSE Have students set a purpose for reading *Let's Surprise Mom*. Remind them of what they learned when previewing the book. If students need help in setting a purpose, ask: What do you want to find out about the surprise?

STRATEGY SUPPORT: BACKGROUND KNOWLEDGE Help students activate background knowledge by setting up a classroom KWL (Know, Want to Know, Learned) chart on the chalkboard. Use students' ideas about baking from the Build Background section as the Know part of the chart. Have students suggest facts they want to know about baking. When students have finished reading, have them fill in the Learned part of the chart with facts about baking from the text.

COMPREHENSION QUESTIONS

PAGES 3–4 Why does James decide to make breakfast for Mom? *(She is always doing nice things for him.)*

PAGE 7 What did James pick up first at the Farmer's Market? *(He bought blueberries.)*

PAGES 9–10 Where does James buy flour, sugar, baking powder, salt, butter, and milk? *(at the grocery store)*

PAGE 11 What might James and Nana do after they leave the grocery store? *(Possible response: They might go home and make the blueberry pancakes for Mom.)*

REVISIT THE BOOK

READER RESPONSE

1. Farmer's market: fruit stands and vendors Both: eggs and fruits Grocery store: flour, butter, milk, baking powder, check out line
2. Responses will vary but should include logical answers using prior knowledge.
3. Possible responses: baseball cards, goods for services (bartering)
4. Possible responses: He could make scrambled eggs. He would need to buy eggs. He could go to the farmer's market or the grocery store.

EXTEND UNDERSTANDING

Remind students that *dialogue*, or speech, is what characters say to each other. Suggest that students look at the dialogue on page 11. When the cashier asks James what he is making, James smiles and says, "A surprise for Mom!" Discuss why James says that and what it shows about his character.

RESPONSE OPTIONS

WRITING Have students make a list of ingredients they would need to make a healthful snack mix. Then have them create a recipe card listing the ingredients and the steps they would take to make the snack mix.

SOCIAL STUDIES CONNECTION

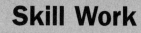

Suggest that students research food or ethnic recipes from other countries. Then invite students to write a short story about going to the market to buy the food they need to prepare the dish.

Skill Work

TEACH/REVIEW VOCABULARY

Have students work in pairs with a set of vocabulary word cards. Have one student pick a card and define the word while the partner uses it in a sentence. Then have partners switch roles as they draw another card.

TARGET SKILL AND STRATEGY

COMPARE AND CONTRAST Tell students that *comparing* means finding similarities between things and *contrasting* mean finding differences. With students, make a chart that compares and contrasts James and Nana.

BACKGROUND KNOWLEDGE Remind students that thinking about what they already know about a topic can help them understand what they read. Explain that activating *background knowledge* can help them see how ideas in the story are alike or different. Remind students of the list compiled of what they already know about baking gathered during the Build Background. As students read, have them take note of how they used this information to help them understand the text.

ADDITIONAL SKILL INSTRUCTION

MAIN IDEA As they read the story, ask students to question what it is mostly about—its *main idea*. Tell students to look for details in the text that support their answers. Model: What is page 4 about? I think it is about James wanting to do something nice for Mom. The details that support my answer are that James agrees with Nana when she suggests that they make breakfast for Mom, and James suggests they make pancakes.

Compare and Contrast

- A **comparison** shows how two or more things are alike. A **contrast** shows how two or more things are different.
- Clue words such as **like** or **as** show comparisons. Clue words such as **but** and **unlike** show contrasts.

Directions Look back at the selection *Let's Surprise Mom.* Using the graphic organizer below, write the facts about grocery shopping and baking under the correct heading.

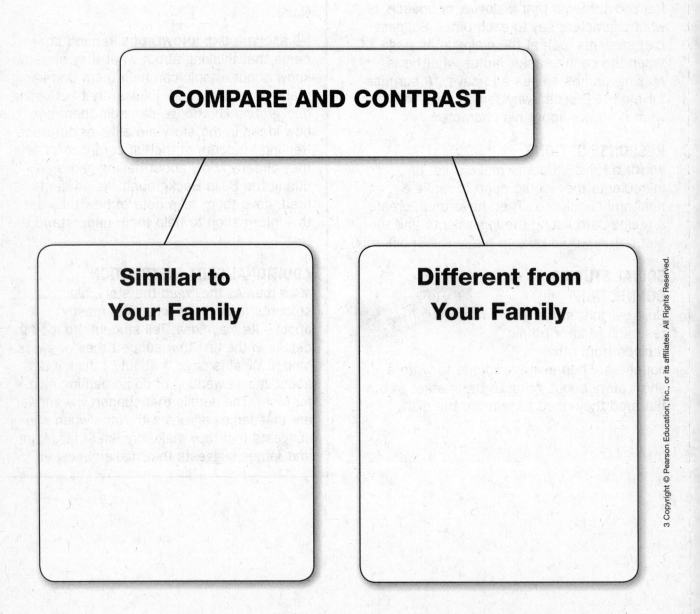

COMPARE AND CONTRAST

Similar to Your Family

Different from Your Family

Vocabulary

Directions Unscramble each word from the box. Then write its definition.

> ## Check the Words You Know
> | | | | |
> |---|---|---|---|
> | ___laundry | ___section | ___shelves | ___spoiled |
> | ___store | ___thousands | ___traded | ___variety |

1. soutsdahn _____

   _____

2. teiscon _____

   _____

3. deislop _____

   _____

4. dalyrun _____

   _____

Directions Complete each sentence. Fill in each blank with the best word from the box.

5. Mom _____ seats with James so that he could sit near the window.

6. The farmer's market offered a _____ of fresh fruit.

7. As James walked down the aisles of the grocery store, he noticed the _____ were filled with all kinds of food.

8. James and Nana went to the grocery _____ to buy other ingredients to make the pancakes.

E-mail Friends

SUMMARY This is a book about two friends from very different cultures and how they keep in touch via e-mail. Through the characters' messages, students can see the differences and similarities in these friends' values and in their cultures. Students can also experience storytelling in a new way—through e-mails.

LESSON VOCABULARY

arranged	bundles
dangerously	errands
excitedly	steady
unwrapped	wobbled

INTRODUCE THE BOOK

INTRODUCE THE TITLE AND AUTHOR Discuss with students the title and the author of *E-mail Friends*. Based on the title, ask students what kind of information they think this book will provide. Ask: Have you ever read a book in e-mail form?

BUILD BACKGROUND Discuss with students if they have ever written letters or sent e-mails to friends or pen pals. Ask: What sorts of things did you write about? Do students know people from different countries? Discuss how they think students from different countries might differ from and be similar to students in the classroom.

PREVIEW/USE ILLUSTRATIONS Have students preview the book by looking at the illustrations. Ask: Where do you think these two e-pals live? (*The girl probably lives in the United States, and the boy lives in Africa.*)

READ THE BOOK

SET PURPOSE Have students set a purpose for reading *E-mail Friends*. Students' curiosity about different countries and their interest in e-mail and computers should guide this purpose.

STRATEGY SUPPORT: STORY STRUCTURE As students read about the two friends getting to know each other, they should follow the story structure to help them keep track of its overall meaning. Following a story from beginning to end will help students distinguish between plot and detail. The story is easy to follow in this book because the actions and ideas are divided into e-mail messages. If you wish, explain to students that telling a story through letters is a very old form of story structure. Ask if students think e-mail is equally old. (*No, because computers, and therefore e-mail, have only been around for a few years.*)

COMPREHENSION QUESTIONS

PAGES 4–5 What are the two main settings in this book? (*Tanzania and Colorado*)

PAGE 6 What is similar about Tanzania and Colorado? (*Possible responses: Soccer is enjoyed in both places; both have wildlife.*)

PAGES 6–7 What does Molly put in her message that makes Juma answer? (*a question*)

PAGES 10–11 How is Molly going to try and make Juma's visit fun? (*Juma wants to see grizzlies, and Molly's father is going to take them to the mountains to look for wildlife.*)

REVISIT THE BOOK

READER RESPONSE

1. Possible responses: To teach students about other cultures. To show differences between countries and cultures.

2. Molly writes to Juma about the giraffe. Juma writes about his father's tour and soccer. Molly writes about American sports and the Fourth of July. Juma writes about a baby zebra.

3. *Excitedly* means "with strong, lively feelings." *Dangerously* means "not safely."

4. Responses will vary but should include a question related to Tanzania.

EXTEND UNDERSTANDING Discuss with students how *plot* refers to the events of the story and always has a beginning, middle, and end. Suggest that students look at both the beginning and the ending of the story and then discuss with students whether Molly and Juma are better friends at the beginning of the story or at the end.

RESPONSE OPTIONS

WRITING Ask students what interests them about where Juma or Molly lives and what else they would like to know about the characters' lives. Then ask students to write e-mails to both Juma and Molly, asking them questions about their homes and their activities. Have volunteers read their e-mails aloud.

SOCIAL STUDIES CONNECTION

Assign each student an imaginary pen pal from another country. Have students research what their e-pals' countries are like. Discuss the things students might like to ask their pen pals and the things they think their pen pals might like to know about life in the United States. Invite students to compose their letters in class. Create a bulletin board where students can post their letters.

Skill Work

TEACH/REVIEW VOCABULARY

Review the vocabulary words with students. Then play "right word, wrong sentence" with students. Take a word like *steady* and use it in two different sentences: *That strong table is steady. The tilted table with the broken leg is steady.* Then ask students to determine in which sentence the word is used correctly. *(the first)* Repeat with all vocabulary words.

TARGET SKILL AND STRATEGY

AUTHOR'S PURPOSE Tell students that the *author's purpose* is the reason or reasons an author has for writing. Common purposes are to persuade, to inform, to entertain, and to express. If an author wants to explain important information, you may want to read slowly. Ask students what information they think the author wanted them to learn and adjust the way they read accordingly.

STORY STRUCTURE Remind students that the *story structure* is how a story is organized, and that a story has a beginning, a middle, and an end. Discuss with students how this story might look different from other stories they have read because it is written as a series of e-mails. Ask students to think about what the beginning, middle, and end might be as they read.

ELL Instruct students to write three different sentences. One sentence will describe the beginning of the story, one will describe the middle, and the last will describe the end.

ADDITIONAL SKILL INSTRUCTION

COMPARE AND CONTRAST Remind students that *comparing* means finding similarities between things and *contrasting* means finding differences. With students, make a chart that compares and contrasts the two characters from the book.

Author's Purpose

- The **author's purpose** is the reason or reasons an author has for writing a story.
- An author may have one or more reasons for writing.

Directions Read the passage below. Then write the answers to the question on the lines.

Dear Molly,
Father found a baby zebra yesterday. She was dangerously far from the herd. Today she wobbled on her tiny legs. Father said she will be more steady each day.
Take care,
Juma

Dear Juma,
I'd like to see that zebra. My dad teaches people about wildlife. He is worried about grizzly bears. People are taking over their habitats.
Well, I'm off to do errands.
Molly

1. Why do you think the author wrote this passage?

_____

_____

2. What is another reason the author may have written the passage?

_____

_____

3. Why do you think the author mentions the jobs of Juma's father and Molly's dad?

_____

_____

4. Why do you think the author uses the words "father" and "dad"?

_____

_____

Vocabulary

Directions Fill in the letters to make each of the words from the box. Then write a definition on the line under the word.

Check the Words You Know

__arranged	__bundles	__dangerously	__errands
__excitedly	__steady	__unwrapped	__wobbled

1. __ R R __ N __ __ D

_____

2. W __ B B __ __ __

_____

3. E __ __ A __ D S

_____

4. E __ C __ __ E __ __ Y

_____

5. __ T __ A D __

_____

6. D __ __ G E __ __ __ S __ Y

_____

7. __ U __ D __ E S

_____

8. __ N __ R __ P P __ __

_____

Directions Write a sentence that includes one of the vocabulary words.

9. _____

_____

The Frozen Continent: Antarctica

SUMMARY Though Antarctica is the coldest place on Earth, it is home to penguins, seals, and other animals. Antarctica is also a fascinating place for scientists who study weather. These scientists measure temperature changes there to understand the effects of air pollution on global climates.

LESSON VOCABULARY

cuddles	flippers
frozen	hatch
pecks	preen
snuggles	

INTRODUCE THE BOOK

INTRODUCE THE TITLE AND AUTHOR Discuss with students the title and the author of *The Frozen Continent: Antarctica*. Ask: What does the cover photo tell you about Antarctica's climate, land, and animals? Discuss what information students think the author will provide based on the title and cover.

BUILD BACKGROUND Invite students to discuss what they know about Antarctica from movies, TV, books, or magazines. Ask: What might you see if you traveled to Antarctica? Does it seem like a place you would want to visit? Why or why not?

PREVIEW/USE TEXT FEATURES Have students look at the pictures, captions, and diagrams to find clues about what aspects of Antarctica will be covered in the book. Point out that certain images, such as snow and penguins, appear often in the pictures.

READ THE BOOK

SET PURPOSE Have students set a purpose for reading *The Frozen Continent: Antarctica*. What impressions do they get from skimming the photos, captions, and maps in the book? What makes Antarctica so different from most other continents? Students' curiosity should guide their purpose for reading.

STRATEGY SUPPORT: MONITOR AND CLARIFY When students *monitor* their comprehension, they should realize when they understand what they're reading and when they do not. There are strategies to restore their understanding when problems arise, such as summarizing facts and details to clarify ideas. Encourage them to read on to see if basic ideas are explained on the next pages. Challenge them to summarize facts and details after they finished reading.

COMPREHENSION QUESTIONS

PAGE 5 What types of animals live in Antarctica? *(penguins, fish, seals, and whales)*

PAGES 6–8 What is the main idea of this section? *(Possible response: Scientists who study the weather in Antarctica use very specialized tools.)*

PAGE 9 How is Antarctica helping scientists learn about climate change? *(Possible response: Its changes in temperature tell about the effects of global warming.)*

REVISIT THE BOOK

READER RESPONSE

1. Possible response: Main idea: Scientists study the climate in Antarctica. Details: They use a radio called an acoustic sounder to find out about wind speed and direction. Weather balloons with radios record information about the air.

2. Responses will vary but students should identify the clarifying strategies they used to resolve their problems and confusion.

3. The words that follow—"or clean and smooth their feathers"—show what *preen* means.

4. Responses will vary.

EXTEND UNDERSTANDING Point out how images in the book are paired together for certain reasons. Ask students what they can learn from such combinations, such as the satellite image paired with the photo of an actual satellite on page 7 and the global warming diagram paired with the photo of a traffic jam on page 9.

RESPONSE OPTIONS

WRITING Ask students to pretend they are visiting Antarctica and writing letters to friends at home. Have them write one or two paragraphs describing their experiences.

WORD WORK On the board, write groups of four words, three of which have similar meanings and one of which is completely opposite or unrelated. Include story vocabulary words in some groups. Have students point out which word in each group does not belong. For example, in the group *frozen*, *icy*, *freezing*, and *melted*, the word *melted* does not belong.

SCIENCE CONNECTION

Scientists in Antarctica use special equipment to gather information. Invite students to learn how scientists in other environments use special tools and technology to gather information.

Skill Work

TEACH/REVIEW VOCABULARY

Discuss the vocabulary words and reinforce word meaning by asking questions such as, "What are some animals that have *flippers?*"

ELL Distribute index cards, each with a vocabulary word written on it. Challenge students to go on a scavenger hunt to find books, magazines, or other print sources containing the same word.

TARGET SKILL AND STRATEGY

MAIN IDEA AND DETAILS Remind students that the *main idea* is the most important idea about a topic. *Supporting details* are pieces of information that tell more about the main idea. Model how asking questions helps readers find the main idea of a book. Ask: In a word or two, what is this book about? (This identifies the topic.) What is the most important idea about the topic? (This identifies the main idea.) What are some details that tell more about the main idea? As students read, have them think about what could be the main idea of the book and what details may support it.

MONITOR AND CLARIFY Remind students that good readers pause occasionally in their reading to be sure they understand what they have read. If needed, students should go back and reread or use any other clarifying strategies that might help.

ADDITIONAL SKILL INSTRUCTION

GENERALIZE Remind students that they are often given ideas about several related things. To make a statement about all of them together is to *generalize* about them. This statement might tell how the things are mostly or completely alike in some way. Have students look for generalizations in the book. Clue words such as *most, many, usually, few, seldom, all,* and *generally* can signal generalizations.

Main Idea and Details

- The **main idea** is the most important idea about a paragraph, passage, article, or book.
- **Details** are pieces of information that support, or tell more about, the main idea.

Directions Read the following passage. What is the main idea of the paragraph? Write it in the box at the top. Then find three details that tell about the main idea. Write one detail in each smaller box.

> Antarctica is very windy and dry. Antarctica is so dry that scientists call it a desert. The small amount of snow that falls there never melts. It is moved around by the wind until it freezes into ice.

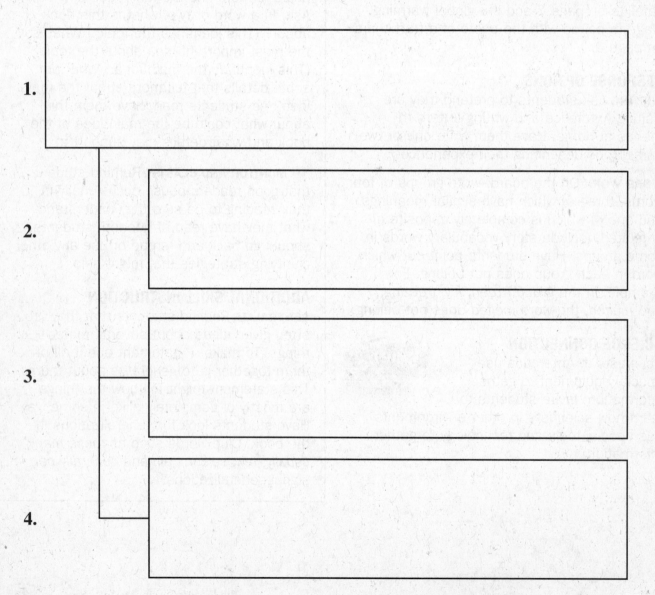

1.

2.

3.

4.

Vocabulary

Directions For each vocabulary word, write the letter of the definition that matches it.

Check the Words You Know

___cuddles   ___flippers   ___frozen   ___hatch

___pecks   ___preen   ___snuggles

---

1. _____ cuddles   **a.** strikes at with the beak

2. _____ flippers   **b.** presses closely against, as for comfort

3. _____ frozen   **c.** to come out of an egg

4. _____ hatch   **d.** hugs closely

5. _____ pecks   **e.** flat body parts that are used for swimming

6. _____ preen   **f.** turned into ice

7. _____ snuggles   **g.** to clean and smooth feathers

Directions Write the vocabulary word or words that go best with each clue.

8. This word describes Antarctica. _____

9. Penguins use these to swim well. _____

10. A penguin chick does this to its eggshell. _____

11. This is another word for how a penguin chick is born. _____

Directions Write a short paragraph. Use at least three of the vocabulary words.

_____

_____

_____

_____

_____

_____

Buddy Goes to School

SUMMARY Buddy, Anna's shelter puppy, needs to learn how to behave better. Anna and her mom take Buddy to puppy school, where Buddy doesn't follow instructions. The teacher tells them to work with Buddy at home too. Buddy graduates with honors.

LESSON VOCABULARY

adorable	compassionate
exactly	iguana
mature	mention
trophies	

INTRODUCE THE BOOK

INTRODUCE THE TITLE AND AUTHOR Discuss with students the title and the author of *Buddy Goes to School*. Ask: Why do people take dogs to school? What kinds of things can dogs learn in school?

BUILD BACKGROUND Ask students if they have ever known a dog that was trained to be well behaved. What did the dog learn to do? Continue the discussion by asking why it is important for pet dogs to be well behaved, especially if they live with a family.

PREVIEW/USE ILLUSTRATIONS Have students skim through the book, looking at the pictures. Ask: What do you think the story is about? Who are the characters? Where does the story appear to take place?

READ THE BOOK

SET PURPOSE Have students set a purpose for reading *Buddy Goes to School*. This purpose should be guided by the impressions students get from reading the title and skimming the illustrations along with their own curiosity.

STRATEGY SUPPORT: VISUALIZE Remind students how to *visualize:* As you read, form pictures in your mind about what is happening in the story. Tell students that they should combine what they already know with details from the text to create pictures in their mind. Add that they can use all of their senses, not just sight, to help them form pictures. Model: On page 3, I see that Buddy is barking and pulling at his leash while the dog next to them is sitting. Anna looks very sad.

COMPREHENSION QUESTIONS

PAGE 5 What is Buddy doing in this illustration? What are the other dogs doing? (*Buddy is still pulling at his leash and barking. The other dogs are sitting quietly.*)

PAGE 6 What is happening between Anna and Buddy? (*She is getting a kiss after she has calmed him down.*)

PAGE 8 Why does Anna's friend Tia think of her pet iguana while she is helping to train Buddy to lie down? (*Possible response: She is thinking how different an iguana is from a cuddly puppy.*)

PAGE 10 Why do you think Buddy got the class trophy for hardest worker? (*The teacher knew that Buddy worked at home as well as in class.*)

REVISIT THE BOOK

READER RESPONSE

1. Buddy: isn't as mature as the other dogs; Other dogs: easier to train; Both: all are dogs and are at a puppy school.
2. Responses will vary based on what students have read and experienced.
3. *Compassionate* is used on page 4. Responses should indicate understanding of both the word and the concept.
4. Responses will vary but should reflect the instructor's suggestions and also the bond that Buddy obviously has with his family.

EXTEND UNDERSTANDING Explore the element of *plot* with students by asking questions such as "What does the author want readers to learn from reading this story?" Have them state the main problem in the story (*Buddy's misbehavior*) and how it is resolved (*loving training in puppy school classes and at home too*).

RESPONSE OPTIONS

WORD WORK Challenge students to write or verbalize sentences that incorporate two or more vocabulary words. Provide an example, such as *When puppy school began, Buddy was adorable but not exactly mature.* Allow them to use the same words in more than one sentence.

SOCIAL STUDIES CONNECTION

Time For SOCIAL STUDIES

Provide appropriate nonfiction books about working dogs and their roles with humans, and invite students to use reference sources to learn more about different types of work that dogs can be trained to do. Have students share what they learn with the class.

Skill Work

TEACH/REVIEW VOCABULARY

Read the vocabulary words. Ask students about words they may already know. Discuss how they first heard of the words and what they think the words mean. Tell them that they will become more familiar with these words as they read.

ELL Using index cards, have students choose a vocabulary word and write it on one side. On the reverse, have each student illustrate his or her word. Then let students exchange cards and guess the correct English words from the illustrations.

TARGET SKILL AND STRATEGY

COMPARE AND CONTRAST Remind students that to *compare* two or more things, they describe how those things are alike. To *contrast* is to describe only how the things are different. Ask students to tell how Buddy is like the other puppies. Then have them state how Buddy is unlike the other puppies. Next have students compare and contrast a puppy with an iguana.

VISUALIZE Tell students that to visualize is to form a picture in their minds about what they are reading. Encourage students to visualize the scenes and characters in *Buddy Goes to School* as they read it. Encourage them to activate all of their senses—hearing, smell, taste, and touch, as well as sight.

ADDITIONAL SKILL INSTRUCTION

SEQUENCE The *sequence* of a story's events is the order in which events occur. Students should use sequence skills to keep track of which events happened first, next, and last for a correct understanding of books such as *Buddy Goes to School.* Have them consider whether Buddy could have "graduated" with the other puppies if he had not worked at home to learn his commands. From the illustrations as well as the text, trace Anna's feelings about Buddy.

Compare and Contrast

- A **comparison** shows how two or more things are alike and different.
- A **contrast** shows how two or more things are different.

Directions Look back at *Buddy Goes to School* to complete the chart. Fill in the information you are given to know about how Buddy and the other puppies act as well as how Tia's pet iguana acts.

Buddy	Other Puppies	Tia's Pet Iguana
1. _____ 2. _____	3. _____	4. _____

5. Write a paragraph explaining why you would or would not like to have a dog like Buddy or an iguana as a pet. Use details from the chart and also from the story as you write.

_____

_____

_____

_____

_____

_____

_____

Vocabulary

Directions Choose the word from the box that best matches each definition. Write the word on the line.

> ## Check the Words You Know
> ___adorable   ___compassionate   ___exactly   ___iguana
> ___mature   ___mention   ___trophies

1. _____ mentally or physically like an adult

2. _____ to speak about

3. _____ attractive, delightful

4. _____ large lizard with a spiny crest on its back

5. _____ prizes awarded to individuals or teams

6. _____ accurate, precisely

7. _____ sympathetic

Directions Write the vocabulary word that completes each sentence.

8. Tia's _____ was not very affectionate.

9. Puppies are usually very cute and _____, even when they misbehave.

10. The instructor passed out _____ to all of the puppies and their owners.

11. People who adopt their pets from shelters are being _____ .

12. A kitten is not a _____ cat, nor is a puppy a grown-up dog.

The Metal Detective

SUMMARY A boy named Joe is bored until his grandmother teaches him how to use a metal detector. Joe has a chance to use the device to find a gold ring that was lost by his grandmother's neighbor. He decides that using the metal detector will be a fun way to stay busy during the summer.

LESSON VOCABULARY

butterflies	collection
enormous	scattered
shoelaces	strain

INTRODUCE THE BOOK

INTRODUCE THE TITLE AND AUTHOR Discuss with students the title and the author of *The Metal Detective*. Ask them to look at the cover illustration and identify the metal detector. For what purposes might the person use a metal detector? How can students tell?

BUILD BACKGROUND Have students discuss times when they or someone they know helped others by coming up with a creative solution to a problem. What was the solution and how did it solve the problem? How did everyone feel afterward?

PREVIEW/USE TEXT FEATURES Read aloud the title and have students glance through the illustrations. Ask students to predict what type of story they will read and what will happen in it based on these features.

READ THE BOOK

SET PURPOSE Have students set a purpose for reading *The Metal Detective* by asking them questions about the title. What do detectives do, and what type of story might have a detective in it? What might a detective be seeking with a metal detector? Ask students to base their answers on previously read books and their own prior knowledge.

STRATEGY SUPPORT: QUESTIONING Remind students that asking good questions about important text information in a story is a good way to become a better reader. Questioning can take place before, during, and after reading a story. After previewing and setting a purpose for reading *The Metal Detective*, encourage students to ask themselves a question to keep in mind as they begin. Model: I wonder what this will be about.

COMPREHENSION QUESTIONS

PAGE 7 How did Ms. Choi lose her gold ring? *(It most likely slipped from her finger while she was working in her garden.)*

PAGE 9 What solution did Joe and Grandma come up with for finding Ms. Choi's ring? Why did it make sense? *(They decided to use the metal detector to find the ring because the ring was made of metal.)*

PAGE 11 What might Joe do with the metal detector later in the summer? *(Possible response: He might find coins for his coin collection or metal cans for recycling.)*

REVISIT THE BOOK
READER RESPONSE

1. Possible response: Joe concluded that he could become a detective with the metal detector. Though he had been bored, he grew interested in this new possibility when he found things such as coins—and the gold ring—in Ms. Choi's garden.

2. Responses will vary but should include reasonable questions about metal detectors such as what items would a metal detector find (toy cars, watches, keys, jewelry, coins)

3. Possible responses: colossal, gigantic, huge, massive

4. Possible responses: They can find sharp objects on lawns before they can harm people. They can help police find evidence in crimes.

EXTEND UNDERSTANDING Tell students that a character is someone who takes part in the events of a story. Then, explain that character traits are the qualities or characteristics of a character. Create a character web based on a person from the book. Then invite students to identify the character's traits and explain their responses with examples. Record these responses on the web.

RESPONSE OPTIONS

WRITING How should Joe spread the word about his services as a metal detector detective? Ask students to write an advertisement that promotes his services.

WORD WORK Provide students with magazines and newspapers and ask them to cut out pictures that show the meanings of the lesson vocabulary words. For example, an image of an elephant may represent the word "enormous." Have students paste their pictures on a separate sheet of paper and, under each image, write the corresponding word. Invite volunteers to share their work.

SCIENCE CONNECTION

TIME FOR Science

Remind students that a metal detector was used to search for a lost metal object in the story. Have students come up with other examples of how specific tools and devices are designed to solve specific problems such as a can opener.

Skill Work

TEACH/REVIEW VOCABULARY

Have volunteers define the vocabulary words and use them in sentences to help classmates improve their understanding of them.

ELL In pairs, have students make up a riddle game using vocabulary words. Suggest an example such as "I have just tied my _____."

TARGET SKILL AND STRATEGY

DRAW CONCLUSIONS Explain to students that an author may have more than one reason for writing a story. *The Metal Detective*, for instance, is a story both about metal detectors and about how Joe overcomes feeling bored. Ask students to tell what they believe is the most important idea behind this story.

QUESTIONING Have students revisit and answer the questions they asked themselves before they began to read *The Metal Detective*. Then have them generate a final question, such as *I wonder what the author wanted me to understand.*

ADDITIONAL SKILL INSTRUCTION

REALISM AND FANTASY Tell students that a *realistic* story tells about something that could happen, and a *fantasy* is a story about something that could not happen. Ask students to identify specific elements within *The Metal Detective* that indicate which type of story it is. Then have them point out previously read books that exemplify the other type of story and explain why.

Draw Conclusions

- When you **draw a conclusion,** you think about facts and details and decide something about them..

Directions Read the following passage about metal detectors. Insert one fact about metal detectors in each fact box, and then see what conclusion you can draw.

A metal detector is an amazing invention. When it is turned on, it makes a beeping sound as it passes over certain kinds of metal. People like to use detectors because with them they can find coins and precious metals such as gold and platinum. Metal detectors are often used on beaches and in parks, where people may lose track of things.

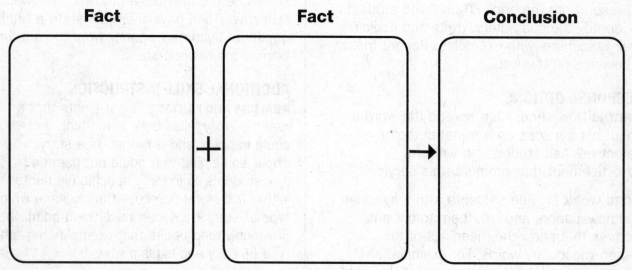

Fact + **Fact** → **Conclusion**

Vocabulary

Directions Draw a line to connect each vocabulary word with the correct description.

Check the Words You Know

___butterflies   ___collection   ___enormous
___scattered   ___shoelaces   ___strain

1. butterflies   **a.** sprinkled

2. collection   **b.** extremely large

3. enormous   **c.** insects, often with brightly colored wings

4. scattered   **d.** struggle

5. shoelaces   **e.** group of things that belong together

6. strain   **f.** strings for fastening shoes

Directions Write the vocabulary word that completes each clue.

7. This word describes the size of something.

_____

8. When you try hard, you do this.

_____

9. If you sprinkled seeds over a flower bed, you might describe the seeds this way.

_____

10. People organize seashells, stamps, dolls, and baseball cards into one of these.

_____

Growing Vegetables

SUMMARY This is a story about a group of kids working together for a common goal: planting and growing a vegetable garden. By taking readers through a busy day in the garden, the story shows how much work goes into growing a garden and how sharing the work is more fun and productive for everyone.

LESSON VOCABULARY

bottom	cheated	clever
crops	lazy	partners
wealth		

INTRODUCE THE BOOK

INTRODUCE THE TITLE AND AUTHOR Discuss with students the title and the author of *Growing Vegetables*. Point out the science content triangle on the cover and ask students how they think this may relate to the selection's title and content.

BUILD BACKGROUND Ask students if they have ever grown plants. Discuss what kind of plants they grew and how they cared for them. If students are interested, begin a discussion about different kinds of gardens, such as herb gardens or flower gardens, or about plants that grow in water or grow without soil.

PREVIEW/USE TEXT FEATURES As students preview the book, point out that illustrations can often help them when they encounter unfamiliar words, terms, or ideas. Direct their attention to page 8, where students will see a drawing of Alex's plant. The illustration helps students figure out what the words *bean plant* mean. Go through the rest of the illustrations with students and see if the drawings relate to any of the words in the text in the same way.

READ THE BOOK

SET PURPOSE Have students set a purpose for reading *Growing Vegetables*. Students' interest in growing vegetables and working together should guide this purpose. Suggest that students think about all that goes into growing the vegetables that they eat at home or see in the supermarket or at farm stands.

STRATEGY SUPPORT: PREDICT As students read about how vegetables grow, *predicting* gives them a chance to use what they already know and to imagine what is going to happen next in the story.

COMPREHENSION QUESTIONS

PAGE 3 Why does the Garden Bunch want to work together to plant a garden? *(They are friends who love to dig in the dirt and who want to sell the vegetables.)*

PAGE 4 Why did the Garden Bunch plant their garden in a sunny spot? *(Vegetables need lots of sunlight to grow.)*

PAGE 7 Can you predict what will happen if Miranda forgets to water the carrots again? *(The carrots will wilt even more.)*

PAGE 10 Using clues in the text, explain what *harvest* means. *(It means to pick or gather.)*

REVISIT THE BOOK

READER RESPONSE

1. Possible response: to inform readers about growing vegetables
2. Possible response: They may plant a new garden. The story says that the kids planted a garden last summer. This summer they grew new plants.
3. Possible response: *busy, lively*
4. Possible response: The plants were planted in rows; the vegetables were planted in separate areas; markers identified each crop.

EXTEND UNDERSTANDING Explain to students that identifying details and facts can help them understand what is important in a story. Discuss with students the facts they learned about growing things from this story. Ask them to write details about how to grow each plant mentioned in the story.

RESPONSE OPTIONS

WRITING Instruct students to look at the illustration of the Garden Bunch's vegetable stand on page 12. Ask them to write a short radio commercial for the stand.

WORD WORK Discuss with students how words like *clever* and *lazy* are adjectives, or descriptive words. Write on the board other adjectives that students know. Then hand out old magazines and ask students to cut out pictures and to write adjectives that describe them. Post pictures in the classroom.

SCIENCE CONNECTION

TIME FOR Science

Students can learn more about measuring by planting a fast-growing plant, such as a sunflower, in the classroom. Every week, ask students to measure the height of the flower as it grows. Suggest that students also track the growth on a weekly chart posted in the classroom.

Skill Work

TEACH/REVIEW VOCABULARY

To reinforce the meaning of the words, ask volunteers to think of a synonym for each word, such as *smart* for *clever*. Then have them think of an antonym for each word.

ELL Ask students to draw pictures that describe each vocabulary word and to write sentences about them.

TARGET SKILL AND STRATEGY

AUTHOR'S PURPOSE Remind students that every author has a *purpose,* or reason, for writing a story. An author may want to entertain, inform, or persuade. Ask students why they think this author wrote this story. Discuss with students what they imagine the author might want them to know about gardening.

PREDICT Remind students that *predicting* is when you guess what is going to happen next in a story based on what has already happened. As students read, remind them to note events that may help them guess what is going to happen next. As students read, suggest that they determine if their predictions were correct. Remind students that predicting is a great way to make sure they understand a story.

ADDITIONAL SKILL INSTRUCTION

GENERALIZE Remind students that a *generalization* is when you recognize similarities and differences about things in a story and come to some conclusion. Clue words such as *all, many, most,* or *never* can help students form generalizations. As students read, have them note any clue words. Ask students if they see common elements in what each gardener does. Suggest that these common elements allow them to make some generalizations about how to garden.

Author's Purpose

- The **author's purpose** is the reason or reasons the author has for writing.
- An author may have one or more reasons for writing. To *inform, persuade, entertain,* or *express* are common reasons.

Directions Answer the questions.

1. Why do you think the author wrote about the time Miranda forgot to water the plants?

   _____

   _____

   _____

2. Why do you think the author told about the special job each person had?

   _____

   _____

   _____

3. Why do you think the author wrote a book about growing vegetables?

   _____

   _____

   _____

4. What do you think the author wanted you to learn about plants?

   _____

   _____

   _____

5. What do you think the author wanted you to learn about working together?

   _____

   _____

   _____

Vocabulary

Directions Circle the letter of the correct definition below each vocabulary word.

Check the Words You Know

___bottom   ___cheated   ___clever   ___crops
___lazy   ___partners   ___wealth

1. lazy
   a. quick   b. not wanting to do any work   c. simple to do

2. crops
   a. big hairy dogs   b. clothing   c. plants or fruits

3. partners
   a. wooden fences   b. people who work together   c. enemies

4. cheated
   a. did not play fairly   b. dressed for dinner   c. destroyed

5. clever
   a. hungry   b. silly   c. smart

6. wealth
   a. dirt   b. money   c. talent

7. bottom
   a. lowest part   b. highest part   c. middle

Directions Unscramble the letters to form a vocabulary word.

8. TAEEHCD _____

9. CREVEL _____

10. TOMBOT _____

11. PRCOS _____

12. PTNSERAR _____

13. ZALY _____

14. HTWEAL _____

All About Birds

SUMMARY In this nonfiction selection, the author describes various birds found around the world. The book describes the many ways that birds are alike and different.

LESSON VOCABULARY

bill	goo
hunters	materials
platform	ton
twigs	

INTRODUCE THE BOOK

INTRODUCE THE TITLE AND AUTHOR Discuss with students the title and the author of *All About Birds*. Have students share what they already know about birds. Based on their responses, talk about the information they think this book will provide.

BUILD BACKGROUND Discuss with students what they know about specific birds such as hummingbirds, eagles, penguins, and toucans. Ask: Where do they live? What do they look like? What do they eat?

PREVIEW/USE TEXT FEATURES Tell students to preview the book by looking at the photos and reading the captions. Ask them to share any impressions they may have about birds based on these features.

ELL Ask students to identify which of the pictured birds they recognize from their home countries.

READ THE BOOK

SET PURPOSE Have students set a purpose for reading *All About Birds*. Have them think back to their answers to the previous sections. Ask them what they would like to learn. Their curiosity should guide their purpose.

STRATEGY SUPPORT: TEXT STRUCTURE Remind students that authors use different *text structures*. They may organize the information in the book by subject matter; by chronological, or time, order; or in another way. Ask: How does the author organize the information in this book? How does this help you understand the selection?

COMPREHENSION QUESTIONS

PAGE 3 How are all birds alike? *(They all lay eggs.)*

PAGES 4–5 Which bird is the smallest? Which bird is the largest? *(the bee hummingbird; the ostrich)*

PAGES 6–7 Which foods do birds eat? *(Birds eat seeds, fruits, insects, earthworms, fish, and small animals.)*

PAGES 8–9 How is an eagle's nest different from other birds' nests? *(Eagles' nests are very large and are made of giant sticks. An eagle's nest has a wide, flat bottom. Other nests are smaller and are made of small twigs and grasses.)*

REVISIT THE BOOK

READER RESPONSE

1. Possible response: Main idea: birds, all of which lay eggs, are very different from one another. Details: birds come in many sizes, eat food that is easy to find, don't have teeth, live all over the world, make different kinds of nests, fly or don't fly.
2. The question identified that the page would be about the foods that birds eat.
3. Materials mean things that the nests are made of. Birds use twigs, grasses, sticks, mud, and goo.
4. Responses will vary but should include facts about birds found in the book.

EXTEND UNDERSTANDING Invite students to look at the photographs. Discuss the similarities and differences in the appearances of the birds, including their sizes and the nests they live in.

RESPONSE OPTIONS

WRITING Ask students to imagine they are bird watching. Have them write a journal entry about which birds they see, where the birds are, and what they are doing.

SCIENCE CONNECTION

TIME FOR Science

Provide nonfiction books that will help students learn more about other birds, their habitats, and their behaviors. Have students choose two or three birds and create charts outlining the information they learn. Then have students share the information with classmates.

Skill Work

TEACH/REVIEW VOCABULARY

Before reading, introduce the vocabulary words and ask students if they recognize any of them. Have volunteers use the words in sentences based on real-life experiences to help others better understand their meaning.

TARGET SKILL AND STRATEGY

MAIN IDEA AND DETAILS Remind students that the main idea is the most important idea about a paragraph, passage, or article. Details that support the main idea tell the reader more about that idea. Ask: What is this book about? (This identifies the topic, birds.) What is the most important idea about this topic? (This identifies the main idea, that birds are very different from one another.) Ask students to list some of the details they have found.

TEXT STRUCTURE Good readers should determine how the writer has organized the information in the selection. Authors use headings, illustrations, and captions to make information easy to find and read. Ask students how the author organized *Birds*.

ADDITIONAL SKILL INSTRUCTION

COMPARE AND CONTRAST Remind students that *comparing and contrasting* are ways of determining how things are alike and how they are different. Create a graphic organizer, and ask students to compare and contrast third grade to second grade. Then suggest that as they read, students make a graphic organizer to compare and contrast the way that birds are alike and different.

Main Idea and Details

- The **main idea** is the most important idea about a paragraph, passage, or article.
- **Details** are small pieces of information that tell more about the main idea.

Directions Read the following paragraph. What is the main idea? Write it in the box on the left. Then find three details that tell about the main idea. Write them in the boxes on the right.

> Birds are fascinating animals. Although all birds lay eggs and have feathers and wings, they are very different from one another. Birds range in size from the tiny bee hummingbird to the 300-pound ostrich. Some birds eat seeds or fruit while others eat animals as big as rabbits. Birds' nests may be small baskets or giant platforms. Birds live all over the world, in all kinds of habitats.

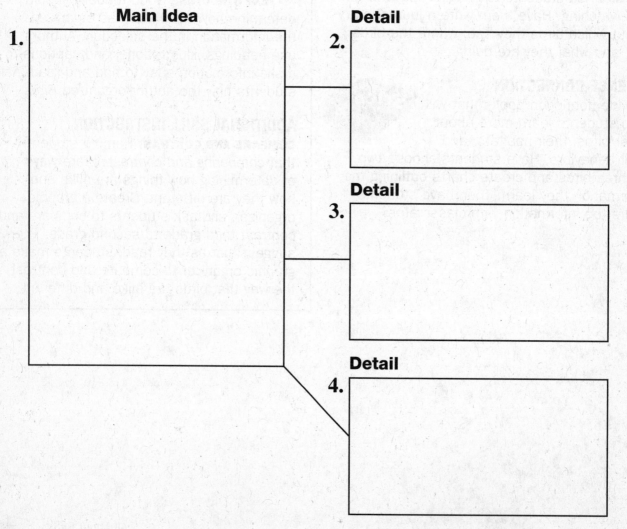

Main Idea

1.

Detail

2.

Detail

3.

Detail

4.

Vocabulary

Directions Write the word or words that best completes each sentence.

Check the Words You Know

___bill	___goo	___hunters	___materials
___platform	___ton	___twigs	

1. An eagle's nest is shaped like a _____.

2. Hawks, eagles, and owls are _____.

3. Birds have two light jaws that form a _____.

4. One eagle's nest can weigh up to a _____.

5. Some _____ that birds use for nests are mud and

_____.

6. _____ and grasses are also used.

Directions Write two or three sentences about how birds build nests. Use as many vocabulary words as possible.

_____

_____

_____

_____

_____

_____

_____

_____

_____

Raisins

SUMMARY Students read about raisins, including how they are made from grapes and how students can make their own raisins.

LESSON VOCABULARY

area	artificial
grapevine	preservative
proof	raise
raisin	

INTRODUCE THE BOOK

INTRODUCE THE TITLE AND AUTHOR Discuss the title and author of *Raisins*. Have students look at the cover and tell what they think the book might be about. Ask them to speculate what fruit raisins are made from. Have them note the science triangle on the cover and ask them how reading about raisins might be scientific.

BUILD BACKGROUND Discuss snack foods with students. Ask them to consider why fruits such as raisins are better for them than other kinds of snacks.

PREVIEW/USE TEXT FEATURES After students have previewed the book, discuss whether the book is fiction or nonfiction and why students think so. As necessary, help them realize that photographs are a clue that tells them this is nonfiction. Ask why they think this is so.

READ THE BOOK

SET PURPOSE Have students set a purpose for reading *Raisins*. Invite them to think about what raisins are made of and how they are made.

STRATEGY SUPPORT: IMPORTANT IDEAS Remind students that good readers recognize which ideas are the most important ones. Explain that as they read they should try to identify the most important ideas. Model questions to ask while reading: Is this idea important enough to remember? Or is this idea just a small detail?

COMPREHENSION QUESTIONS

PAGES 4–5 How do grapes become raisins? *(The grapes are dried in the sun.)*

PAGE 7 Why do you think raisins are better for you than candy or cookies? *(They are a fruit, so they are all natural and they have iron and B vitamins.)*

PAGE 9 Why do you think astronauts take raisins when they go into space? *(Raisins aren't messy and they can go anywhere as a snack food.)*

PAGE 12 When you make raisins, why will you have to wait longer if there have been cloudy days? *(Without a lot of sun, grapes take longer to dry.)*

REVISIT THE BOOK

READER RESPONSE

1. Possible responses: Conclusion: Raisins are easy to make. Evidence: The photographs show the steps; Rinse a bunch of seedless grapes; Put individual grapes on a dish in the sunlight and leave them there until they look like raisins.
2. Important ideas include that raisins are dried grapes and that they are easy to make.
3. Responses may vary, but students should be able to use context clues and the base word *preserve* to figure out that a *preservative* is something that keeps or preserves food.
4. Possible responses: Raisins in oatmeal or oatmeal cookies with raisins.

EXTEND UNDERSTANDING Explain that writers of directions often include illustrations to help readers figure out what to do and see what things should look like at each step. Discuss with students how the photographs of making their own raisins helped them understand the steps.

RESPONSE OPTIONS

SPEAKING Help students understand why candy and cookies are not healthful snacks. Invite small groups to brainstorm a list of healthful snacks that are better for them than candy or cookies. Ask groups to share their lists in a class discussion.

ELL Invite students from other countries to tell about the kinds of snack foods people eat in their countries. Ask whether in those countries they eat raisins or other dried fruit as snacks.

SCIENCE CONNECTION

TIME FOR Science

Point out to students that grapes are not the only fruit that people eat dried. Encourage them to do some research to discover examples of other dried fruits or vegetables, such as apricots, figs, pears, tomatoes, and so on. Have them share their results in a class discussion.

Skill Work

TEACH/REVIEW VOCABULARY

Use each vocabulary word in an oral sentence. Have students use that context to determine the meaning of the word and what part of speech it is.

TARGET SKILL AND STRATEGY

DRAW CONCLUSIONS Remind students that they can use facts and details that they have read and what they already know to figure out something or make a decision while they are reading. Model drawing conclusions with page 9: I know that raisins are a snack food that is good for people. I also know that spaceships don't have much room inside. Help students conclude that raisins are a healthful snack that fits easily into a spaceship.

IMPORTANT IDEAS Remind students that when they read, they should pick out the most important ideas. Help students work with page 4 to identify the first and fourth sentences as the important ideas on the page. Discuss with students why they think these are the important ideas.

ADDITIONAL SKILL INSTRUCTION

GENERALIZE Explain to students that generalizing is like drawing a conclusion, except that a generalization is an idea that is true for many examples. Discuss the features of the directions for making raisins on pages 10–12. Can students generalize that all directions include steps that tell what to do first, next, and last? What other generalizations can they make about written directions? (Possible response: they are usually illustrated.)

Draw Conclusions

- **Drawing conclusions** means using what you read and what you already know to make reasonable decisions about something.

Directions Read the following passage. Then fill in the boxes with facts from the passage and things you already know that are related to those facts. Finally, write the conclusions you can draw from the facts plus what you already know.

Raisins have been made from grapes for more than 4,000 years. In some ancient countries, raisins were sometimes given as prizes in sports contests.

In the United States, the state of California is the only place where grapes for raisins are grown and raisins are made. More raisins are produced there than anywhere else in the world. Australia ranks second in producing raisins.

Fact	What I Know	Conclusion

Fact	What I Know	Conclusion

Name _____

Vocabulary

Directions Write the word that best completes each sentence.

Check the Words You Know

___area   ___artificial   ___grapevine   ___preservative
___proof   ___raise   ___raisin

1. Sometimes raisins are used as a _____ in foods.

2. If you need to prove something is true, you need _____.

3. When farmers grow a crop, they _____ it.

4. A dried grape is called a _____.

5. Grapes need to be dried in a sunny _____.

6. The opposite of natural is _____.

7. A _____ has grapes on it.

Directions Write two or three sentences about raisins using as many vocabulary words as possible.

_____

_____

_____

_____

_____

The Hunters and the Elk

SUMMARY This book introduces students to the Snohomish people and tells how they created their own myth for how and why the Big Dipper is in the sky. The book invites students to think about why and how stories are created and passed down.

LESSON VOCABULARY

antlers	imagined
languages	narrator
overhead	poke

INTRODUCE THE BOOK

INTRODUCE THE TITLE AND AUTHOR Discuss with students the title and the author of *The Hunters and the Elk*. Based on the title, ask students what kind of information they think this book will provide. Ask them what they imagine the people on the cover are doing and why they might be looking at the stars. Encourage them to support their answer with clues in the illustrations.

BUILD BACKGROUND Discuss with students what they know about the constellations and the stars. Ask students if they have ever stargazed, seen a shooting star, or looked through a telescope. Ask: What do you think about when you look at a star or wish upon it?

PREVIEW/USE TEXT FEATURES Invite students to take a picture walk through the illustrations. Ask how the illustrations give clues to the meaning of the story. Discuss with students which illustrations seem realistic and which seem like fantasy, and why.

READ THE BOOK

SET PURPOSE Have students set a purpose for reading *The Hunters and the Elk*. Their curiosity about the stars, myths, and Native American culture should guide this purpose. Suggest that as students read, they take notes to summarize the story and to provide answers for any questions they might have about the stars, myths, or Native American culture.

STRATEGY SUPPORT: INFERRING Explain to students the *inferring* is using information they already know and combining it with information in the text to form their own ideas about the text. Model making an inference about the Snohomish languages using page 5. Say: I read that the Creator gave his leftover languages to the Snohomish people. I know that it is difficult to understand other languages. I can infer that the Snohomish people had a difficult time understanding each other.

COMPREHENSION QUESTIONS

PAGE 3 Summarize why the elk are important to the Snohomish. (*They give meat for food; their skin is used for clothing; and tools, weapons, and art are made from their antlers.*)

PAGE 6 Can you imagine a reason why the Creator had not made the sky high enough? (*Possible responses: The Creator was busy and forgot; the Creator wanted the people to work together to push the sky up.*)

PAGE 9 What was the author's purpose in writing about why the elk were important? (*To explain why the Snohomish would name a constellation after them.*)

PAGE 11 How does this story prove that it's important to work together? (*That's how the Snohomish were able to lift the sky.*)

REVISIT THE BOOK

READER RESPONSE

1. Characters: The Snohomish people, the elk, the hunters, and the Creator; Setting: Washington State; Plot: The sky was too low. The Snohomish people decided to push the sky higher. They raised the sky together.
2. Responses will vary, but should include prior knowledge and text from story.
3. Possible responses: I could look at the other words around it. I could look it up in a dictionary.
4. Possible response: Instead of the hunters chasing elk, they would probably be chasing another animal.

EXTEND UNDERSTANDING Remind students that *sequence* is the order in which story events happen. Have students write the sequence of events in *The Hunters and the Elk.* Ask: How might the story be different if any of the events were shuffled around? Invite students to change the events and write a new myth.

RESPONSE OPTIONS

WRITING Introduce students to a variety of different myths and then suggest that they write their own myth about the Big Dipper. Have students present their myths to the class.

SCIENCE CONNECTION

Provide or have students choose a constellation to research. Encourage them to use the library or the Internet. Then have students either draw their constellation or create one using black paper and white chalk. Remind them to draw lines between the stars to create pictures. Have students share their findings with the class.

Skill Work

TEACH/REVIEW VOCABULARY

To reinforce the contextual meaning of *overhead* on page 4, discuss with students how the phrase "in the night sky" helps to guess the meaning of *overhead.* Do this with the other vocabulary words in the story.

TARGET SKILL AND STRATEGY

CHARACTER, PLOT, AND SETTING Share with students that a *character* is a person who takes part in the events of the story. Ask students to identify two characters in the story. Then explain that the *plot* is the sequence of events that take place in a story from the beginning to the middle to the end. Ask students to tell the plot of the story by reviewing the events in sequence. Tell students the *setting* is where the story takes place. Ask students how the story would be different if it took place in a different setting.

INFERRING Remind students that as they read, they should think about information from the text along with what they already know. Students can use this information to form their own ideas about the text. Have students infer how the Snohomish solved their problems using pages 6, 9, and 11. *(Possible response: The sky was to low. The Snohomish people decided to raise the sky. They worked together to accomplish this task.)*

ELL Ask students to summarize what they did yesterday. Have them provide one main idea and three supporting details.

ADDITIONAL SKILL INSTRUCTION

THEME Without using the word *theme*, remind students that every story has one big idea or lesson. Discuss with students the themes of familiar stories like *The Ant and the Grasshopper. (prepare for the future)* Ask students how that big idea teaches them a lesson.

Character, Plot, and Setting

- A **character** is a person who takes part in events in the story.
- The **plot** is the sequence of events that take place in a story from the beginning to the middle to the end.
- The **setting** is where the story takes place.

Directions Fill in the following information about *The Hunters and the Elk.*

1. Title: _____

2. This story is about _____
(name of characters)

3. This story takes place _____
(where and when)

Beginning　　　　　Middle　　　　　End

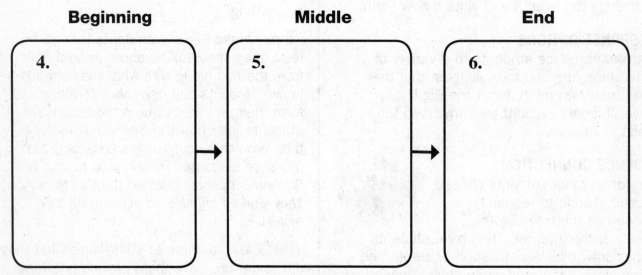

4.　　　　　**5.**　　　　　**6.**

Directions Complete the diagram above. Write two events in each box to tell what happened in *The Hunters and the Elk.* Then answer the questions that below.

7. What is the important message of the story?

_____

_____

8. How would the story have changed if the Creator was not in the story?

_____

_____

Vocabulary

Directions Circle the best definition for each word below. Then use the word in a sentence.

```
┌─────────────────────────────────────────────────────────┐
│              Check the Words You Know                    │
├─────────────────────────────────────────────────────────┤
│  ___antlers        ___imagined        ___languages       │
│  ___narrator       ___overhead        ___poke            │
└─────────────────────────────────────────────────────────┘
```

1. antlers

    a. the horns on an animal's head

    b. the sharp hoofs of an animal

2. _____

_____

3. imagined

    a. laughed very loudly

    b. formed a mental image

4. _____

_____

5. languages

    a. the words people use to communicate

    b. the way people sing

6. _____

_____

7. overhead

    a. above

    b. on the same level

8. _____

_____

Pictures in the Sky

SUMMARY This selection highlights how students can learn to identify stars in the night sky. Information is given about the Big Dipper, Polaris or the North Star, and the Little Dipper.

LESSON VOCABULARY

dim	gases
gigantic	ladle
patterns	shine
temperature	

INTRODUCE THE BOOK

INTRODUCE THE TITLE AND AUTHOR Discuss with students the title and author of *Pictures in the Sky*. Ask: Based on the cover photograph and title, what do you think the book might be about? Direct students' attention to the Science triangle on the cover and ask them how they imagine observing the night sky might be scientific.

BUILD BACKGROUND Ask students if they have ever gazed up at the night sky and found shapes in the stars. Discuss with students what they recall about that experience.

PREVIEW/USE TEXT FEATURES Have students look at the headings and illustrations for the star patterns in this selection. Point out the unique way in which the headings are paired along with illustrations. Why might the author have chosen this arrangement? How might it relate to the book's title?

READ THE BOOK

SET PURPOSE Have students set a purpose for reading *Pictures in the Sky*. Students' interest and curiosity about star patterns should guide this purpose.

STRATEGY SUPPORT: TEXT STRUCTURE Tell students that there are several ways to organize a text—for example, sequence of events, comparison and contrast, description, or definition. Because the text provides facts and characteristics, readers come to understand the main idea through paying attention to the descriptions and sensory details.

COMPREHENSION QUESTIONS

PAGE 4 What conclusions can you make about the best time to find star patterns in the night sky? *(when the sky is clear and there are no clouds)*

PAGE 7 How does the Big Dipper look different in the fall and in winter? *(In winter the dipper's handle points down toward earth; in the fall the ladle is right side up.)*

PAGE 12 Why do you think people create shapes or patterns in the stars? *(Possible response: People can better understand the stars with shapes they are familiar with.)*

REVISIT THE BOOK

READER RESPONSE

1. Possible response: The pictures helped me visualize the different positions of the Big Dipper.
2. Big Dipper: easiest to find, called a big spoon; Little Dipper: dim, called a little spoon; Same: seven stars, both are constellations, Polaris, made of stars or gases
3. Responses will vary but should reflect the meaning of the word *shine*.
4. Responses will vary but should show an understanding of constellations.

EXTEND UNDERSTANDING Explain that authors often include illustrations in nonfiction books to help readers understand what happens in the text. Discuss with students how the pictures of the star patterns in this selection helped them better understand the shapes that the stars make.

RESPONSE OPTIONS

WRITING Invite students to imagine that they discovered a new star pattern and were able to name it. Have them write a journal entry describing what they saw and why they decided to give it its name. Student may want to draw their new star pattern as part of their journal entry.

SCIENCE CONNECTION

Suggest that students research other star patterns not included in this selection. Ask students to draw the patterns on a piece of paper without labeling them. Challenge students to guess what the pattern is. Post the drawings around the room.

Skill Work

TEACH/REVIEW VOCABULARY

Review vocabulary words with students. Then write their meanings on flash cards and challenge students to tell you the vocabulary word that matches each meaning.

ELL After reviewing vocabulary words with students, make two sets of index cards: one with the words and the other with their definitions. Have students match each word to the right definition.

TARGET SKILL AND STRATEGY

GRAPHIC SOURCES Tell students that graphs or charts can help organize the ideas they read. Invite students to make a KWL chart using prior knowledge. Before reading, have them fill in the first section, "What I Know," and the second section, "What I Want to Know." Suggest as students read, they fill in the last section, "What I Learned." Remind students that using graphic sources can help them determine the plot and the big idea of the story.

TEXT STRUCTURES Review with students that *text structure* shows how the book is organized and is a way to find the main idea. Call attention to the heads, photographs, and captions. These elements help students gain significant information, and understand more about the constellations.

ADDITIONAL SKILL INSTRUCTION

AUTHOR'S PURPOSE Remind students that the *author's purpose*, such as to inform, to entertain, to persuade, or to express feelings, is the reason an author writes a selection. Ask students what they imagine this author wants them to know about stars.

Graphic Sources

- **Graphic sources** present information visually and can help you better understand the text.
- Graphic sources include, maps, photographs and captions, time lines, diagrams, graphs, and charts.

Directions Compare and contrast the Big and Little Dipper to the Polairs. Use the chart below for your answers.

Big and Little Dipper	Polaris

Vocabulary

Directions Complete each sentence with a word from the box.

Check the Words You Know

____dim   ____gases   ____gigantic
____ladle   ____patterns   ____shine
____temperature

---

1. The _____ spoon in the sky is the Big Dipper.

2. Some stars in the Little Dipper are _____, or not very bright.

3. The burning _____ gives stars their glow.

4. Polaris is made up of gases that burn at a very high _____.

5. The star pattern of the Big Dipper looks like a giant _____.

6. Many stars _____ very brightly in the night sky.

7. Ancient people saw _____ of stars and named them.

Directions Select four vocabulary words and use each in a sentence.

8. _____

_____

9. _____

_____

10. _____

_____

11. _____

_____

Rescuing Whales

SUMMARY This book introduces the basic concepts surrounding beached, or stranded, whales. Steps of a rescue are described, including how whales are returned to the sea.

LESSON VOCABULARY

anxiously	bay
blizzards	channel
chipped	melodies
supplies	surrounded
symphonies	

INTRODUCE THE BOOK

INTRODUCE THE TITLE AND AUTHOR Discuss with students the title and the author of *Rescuing Whales.* Ask students what they know about whales or any animals in trouble.

BUILD BACKGROUND Most students have not seen a beached whale, but many know about this situation from films or television. Tell students that they will read about keeping a whale alive during its rescue. As they read, suggest that students watch for the first actions of a rescue and determine why they are important to the whale's safety.

PREVIEW/USE TEXT FEATURES Tell students to look at the photographs, map, and journal time line. Ask: What do you notice in the photographs about the people watching the rescue? Draw attention to the journal time line on pages 10–11, and ask students to predict why a whale rescue follows a schedule.

ELL Invite students to share any experiences they may have had with animal rescue or a close call they have had with a sick or injured animal.

READ THE BOOK

SET PURPOSE Most students will be interested in reading this book so that they can learn why whales beach and how to help a beached whale.

STRATEGY SUPPORT: TEXT STRUCTURE While students read *Rescuing Whales,* ask them to fill out a graphic organizer, listing the chain of events in the story. Remind students that not all events are important and need to be listed.

COMPREHENSION QUESTIONS

PAGE 4 Why is it important to immediately cool a beached whale? *(Its body temperature can become very high.)*

PAGE 7 Why don't scientists know what causes a whale to strand? *(Many possible causes make it difficult to pin down one.)*

PAGES 8–11 What happened when three young pilot whales beached themselves in Massachusetts? *(Scientists decided to take the whales to the aquarium, where they healed and adjusted to aquarium life until they were ready to be returned to the sea.)*

PAGE 11 Why do scientists find a pod of whales before lowering a whale into the water? *(Young whales need to be with other and older whales for survival.)*

REVISIT THE BOOK

READER RESPONSE

1. Possible response: Like whales, dolphins need to be directed into deep water.
2. The journal is organized by time. The journal uses A.M. and P.M. The author tells first about draining the water in the aquarium tank so that the young whales can be lifted out.
3. Possible response: gathered around or encircled
4. three hours

EXTEND UNDERSTANDING Ask: Did photographs draw you into this book more quickly than illustrations would have? How is a rescue more meaningful if you can see real people in action? (Possible response: The reader can often identify more with what's going on in the text.)

RESPONSE OPTIONS

WRITING Tell students to pretend they are scientists who specialize in whales. Ask them to write about how they would handle a rescue. Encourage them visit the library and browse the Internet. Their research should help them include facts about why the whale stranded and what the effects of the rescue might be on the whale.

SCIENCE CONNECTION

Suggest that students have a "Humans Care for Animals" day. Volunteers can bring in photos or drawings of the many ways humans can help animals. Make captions for each photo or drawing, and display them in the classroom.

Skill Work

TEACH/REVIEW VOCABULARY

Ask students why this book about whale rescue features words such as *anxiously*, *melody*, and *symphony*. The title shows that a whale is in trouble, which is a reason to be anxious; whales are known to sing playful or mournful melodies. Ask students to look at the other vocabulary words and predict their use in a book about rescuing a whale. Use a map to deal with the geographical or weather-related words.

TARGET SKILL AND STRATEGY

GENERALIZE After reading about a typical whale rescue scene, students should have a general idea of what is involved in helping a stranded whale. Remind students that a *generalization* is a broad statement or rule that applies to many examples. A good place to practice generalizing may be to read over the time line and make statements about the ways people help keep whales alive and safe while they return them to the sea. (Scientists use ships to carry the whales back to pods in deep waters and then finally lower them into the water from special cages.)

TEXT STRUCTURE Explain to students that *text structure* is the way a story is organized. This story tells events in sequence, or in the order they happened. Prompt students to map out the story's chain of events in a graphic organizer during or after reading. Point out that recognizing a story's structure can help students identify cause-and-effect relationships.

ADDITIONAL SKILL INSTRUCTION

SEQUENCE Remind students that understanding sequence, the order of events, can help them keep track of what is going on in the text. In this case, a sequence is graphically displayed in the journal time line on pages 10–11. Students may also read about the events from page 8 on and put them in order, leading up to the day's events when the whales were returned to sea.

Generalize

- When authors present one statement about many ideas or people, they **generalize**.
- A generalization is a kind of conclusion.

Directions Choose one of the generalizations from *Rescuing Whales* listed below. Write the generalization in the top rectangle of the graphic organizer. Then find at least three facts in the story that support the generalization. Write those facts in the boxes below the generalization.

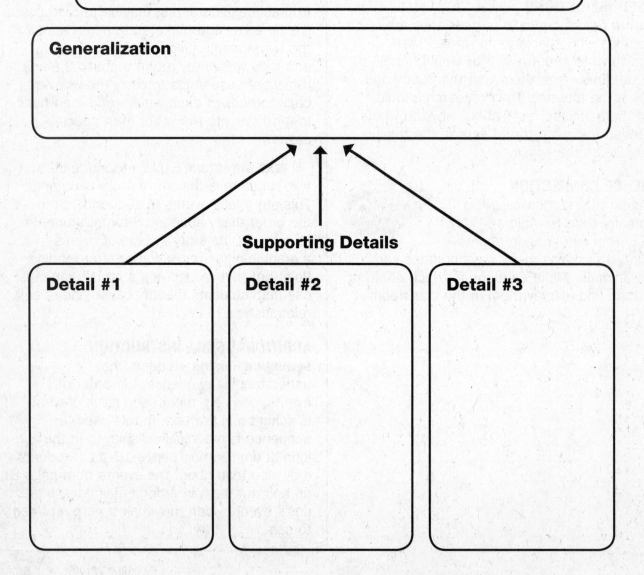

Possible Generalizations

A stranded whale is in great danger unless it is rescued.

There are many things to do to help a stranded whale.

There are many steps in bringing a stranded whale to an aquarium.

Generalization

Supporting Details

Detail #1

Detail #2

Detail #3

Vocabulary

Directions Read the groups of words in each box. Write the vocabulary word that fits with each group.

Check the Words You Know

___ anxiously	___ bay	___ blizzards
___ channel	___ chipped	___ melodies
___ supplies	___ surrounded	___ symphonies

---

1. broken   bits   pieces

_____

2. partly enclosed body of water
   cove   inlet

_____

3. tunes   songs   music

_____

4. deep water   basin   body of water

_____

5. encircled   enclosed   enveloped

_____

6. nervously   fearfully   with panic

_____

7. snowstorms   storms
   heavy snowfalls

_____

8. collection   necessary things
   reserve

_____

9. musical compositions   concerts
   classical music

_____

The Field Trip

SUMMARY In this fictional selection, students read about a class field trip to the real Arizona-Sonora Desert Museum near Tucson, Arizona.

LESSON VOCABULARY

lofty	incredible
noble	search
sting	survivors
topic	unseen
waterless	

INTRODUCE THE BOOK

INTRODUCE THE TITLE AND AUTHOR Discuss the title and author of *The Field Trip*. Have students look at the cover illustration and tell where they think the field trip is taking place.

BUILD BACKGROUND Invite students to briefly discuss the kinds of places they have visited on field trips. Have students share what kinds of animals and plants they have seen on those trips.

PREVIEW/USE TEXT FEATURES Have students preview the book by paging through it and looking at the illustrations. Encourage students to read the title on page 12 and speculate what might be different about that page.

READ THE BOOK

SET PURPOSE Have students set a purpose for reading *The Field Trip*. Suggest that they consider their own field trips as they read the book.

STRATEGY SUPPORT: PREDICT AND SET PURPOSE Remind students that they can be better readers if they predict what a book will be about and decide their purpose for reading it. Point out that they can use titles and illustrations to help them predict what a book will be about. After they have made their predictions, they can consider what their purpose will be. For example, predicting what *The Field Trip* will be about can help them realize they will learn about desert plants and animals.

COMPREHENSION QUESTIONS

PAGES 4–5 What part of the United States do you think Matt lives in? Why do you think so? (*He must live near or in the Sonoran Desert, since the Desert Museum is only about an hour from his school.*)

PAGES 5–6 Why do you think Matt wore sunblock and a hat and brought water? (*These are good things to do whenever you visit a desert.*)

PAGE 8 Do you think Matt was smart to write notes about the lizard he saw? Why or why not? (*Yes, because his notes could help him write the report about what he saw at the museum.*)

PAGE 11 Do you predict that Matt's class will take a field trip to the Arctic? What makes you think so? (*Possible response: No, because they all live much too far away from the Arctic.*)

PAGE 12 How is this page different from the others? (*It is nonfiction and tells facts about the desert instead of telling part of a story.*) Why do you think the author included it? (*to tell more facts*)

REVISIT THE BOOK

READER RESPONSE

1. He left his pencil on the school bus. That caused him to miss the beginning of his class tour. It also helped him observe the lizard and start taking notes for his report.
2. Predictions may vary, but students should consider ideas from the story as topics such as Arctic animals and how they live, how animals and plants are connected, and how they have adapted to the surroundings.
3. Possible response: The word survivors on page 11 means people or animals who can live in difficult conditions.
4. Responses will vary but should reflect students' ideas of what they want to learn about.

EXTEND UNDERSTANDING Tell students that all animals and plants adapt, or change, to be able to survive in their surroundings. Different kinds of animals and plants live in different climates. Invite students to compare the kinds of animals and plants that live in their area to a different one.

ELL Invite students from other countries to describe the kinds of animals and where they lived in these countries. Ask: How are those animals and plants different from those where they live now? How are they different from those in the book?

RESPONSE OPTIONS

WRITING Have students do some research to find out what other kinds of animals live in the desert in addition to lizards, owls, and rabbits. Ask them to write several sentences to describe two or three other desert animals.

SCIENCE CONNECTION

TIME FOR Science

Provide a world map that shows climates. Help students locate several other deserts. Have small teams each choose one of these deserts as the topic for some research. Ask teams to report to the whole class what they discovered about their topic, especially the animals and plants that live there.

Skill Work

TEACH/REVIEW VOCABULARY

Write on the board the vocabulary words *lofty, unseen, survivor,* and *waterless.* Explain that each of these words includes a prefix or suffix. Work with students to identify the suffix *-y* in *lofty,* prefix *un-* in *unseen,* suffix *-or* in *survivor,* and suffix *-less* in *waterless.* Discuss the meanings of the base words and the affixes. Note that *incredible* has a embedded prefix *(in-)* and suffix *(-ible),* so the base *(cred)* is unknown to students.

TARGET SKILL AND STRATEGY

CAUSE AND EFFECT Remind students that a *cause* is why something happens and an *effect* is what happens. For example, because Matt sat on the bench, he saw the lizard. Explain that understanding cause and effect can help students become better readers.

PREDICT AND SET PURPOSE Discuss with students what they predicted *The Field Trip* would be about and their purpose for reading. Ask whether their predictions were correct or if they had to change them as they read. Point out that good readers change their purpose for reading and predictions as they read.

ADDITIONAL SKILL INSTRUCTION

GENERALIZE Explain to students that they can make a generalization about ideas, characters, or situations. A *generalization* is an idea that covers many things that are alike in some way. For example, a generalization about plants and animals is they adapt to their surroundings. Ask students to make a generalization about the other kids in Matt's class. *(They all remembered to take their pencils when they left the bus.)*

Cause and Effect

- A **cause** is why something happens.
- An **effect** is what happens.

Directions Think about the story *The Field Trip*. Match each cause from the story with its effect. Write the letter of the effect next to its cause. Each cause has only one effect.

Causes	Effects
1. The class was beginning a unit on deserts. _____	**a.** Matt realized he left his pencil on the bus.
2. The school was not far from the Desert Museum. _____	**b.** Matt took notes about a lizard he saw.
3. The sun beat down on the kids. _____	**c.** Matt took notes about the owl in the cactus.
4. Ms. Perez told the class to take notes. _____	**d.** Matt wrote such a good report that the class applauded.
5. Matt ran back to the bus to get his pencil. _____	**e.** They went on a field trip to the Desert Museum.
6. Matt sat on a bench to wait for his teacher. _____	**f.** Matt missed the first part of the museum.
7. Matt saw a big cactus with a hole in it. _____	**g.** The bus trip to the Museum took an hour.
8. Matt discovered he had taken lots of notes. _____	**h.** Matt was glad he wore sunblock.

Vocabulary

Directions After each word or phrase below, write the vocabulary word that has the same meaning. Use each word once.

> ## Check the Words You Know
>
> ___lofty   ___incredible   ___noble   ___search
> ___sting   ___survivors   ___topic   ___unseen
> ___waterless

1. what something is about _____

2. high up _____

3. pierce or hurt a little _____

4. unbelievable _____

5. excellent or magnificent _____

6. hidden or behind the scene _____

7. without water; dry _____

8. to look carefully _____

9. those who live in difficult conditions _____

Directions Write two or three sentences about the desert using as many vocabulary words as possible.

_____

_____

_____

_____

The Winning Point!

SUMMARY Although she is a good soccer player otherwise, Lucy freezes up when she's near enough to the goal to score. She learns to focus only on herself and the ball and solves her problem.

LESSON VOCABULARY

basketball	disease
freeze	guard
popular	sports
study	terrible

INTRODUCE THE BOOK

INTRODUCE THE TITLE AND AUTHOR Discuss the title and author of *The Winning Point!* Invite students to look at the illustration and decide what game the book is about and what they think will happen. Ask: Why do you think the author added an exclamation point to the title?

BUILD BACKGROUND Make sure students know something about the game of soccer. Ask volunteers who are players to briefly explain the game to those who don't know about it, or do it yourself if necessary.

PREVIEW/USE TEXT FEATURES Ask students to preview the book by paging through it and looking at the illustrations. Lead them to forecast what the book might be about. Ask why they think page 12 is different.

READ THE BOOK

SET PURPOSE Make sure students consider what they saw when they previewed the book to help them set a purpose for reading.

STRATEGY SUPPORT: SUMMARIZE Discuss with students that *summarizing* means telling only the main ideas or events in a story, not the details. Summarizing is one way good readers check their understanding of what they have read. In a summary, students should tell the main points of a story in their own words.

ELL Work with students as a group to write a summary of the story together. Then edit it to get rid of the unnecessary details. Help them understand the difference between the main ideas and the details.

COMPREHENSION QUESTIONS

PAGES 3–4 What is Lucy's problem? (*She's a good soccer player but never scores, even when she has the chance.*)

PAGE 5 Lucy kicked the ball into the goal when she was chatting with Isabel. Why can't she do that in a game? (*She says she freezes up.*)

PAGES 6–7 What did Lucy do to try to solve her problem? (*She went to the library and found a book by a popular soccer player, who wrote that she, too, had often panicked until she learned to focus.*)

PAGES 10–11 What did Lucy tell herself when she had an opportunity to kick for a goal? (*it was just her and the ball*) How did this help her? (*She was able to focus only on what she was doing, and she made the goal and won the game.*)

PAGE 12 Do you think soccer is the most popular game in the United States? Why or why not? (*Answers will vary, but many students will think that baseball or American football is the most popular game here.*)

REVISIT THE BOOK

READER RESPONSE

1. Possible responses: soccer players work hard; that some freeze; they enjoy playing the game.
2. Possible responses: Lucy is never able to score in soccer; she thinks she should quit; she reads about a famous soccer player who needed to learn to focus; Lucy takes that advice; she kicks the final goal to win a game.
3. Responses will vary but should show an understanding of the vocabulary words.
4. Sentences will vary, but students should follow the directions.

EXTEND UNDERSTANDING Tell students that soccer was not known very well or played much in this country for many years. Only since the 1980s has the game become really popular here. That is one reason many adults do not know the game and it is not seen on television as much as other sports such as baseball or American football.

RESPONSE OPTIONS

ART/LANGUAGE ARTS Invite students to brainstorm a list of their own favorite sports, including those they themselves like to play. Divide students into groups according to their favorite sport. Have each group choose a way to tell the rest of the class about their sport. They may choose to orally describe it, to draw individual pictures, or to work together to create a mural illustrating it.

SPORTS CONNECTION

If possible, have students play a game of soccer on the school grounds or in the gym. Briefly explain the rules of the game before they get started, and divide students into teams. Let everyone have a chance to play.

Skill Work

TEACH/REVIEW VOCABULARY

List on the board the vocabulary words with the pages where they appear: *basketball 5, disease 5, freeze 5, guard 3, popular 6, sports 6, study 6, terrible 5.* Have students find each word, read the sentence in which it appears, and use context clues to decide what it means.

TARGET SKILL AND STRATEGY

GENERALIZE Recall with students that when they make a broad statement that covers many different examples, they are generalizing. Give students several examples, such as *Many kids like to play soccer* or *Most kids at the park play basketball.* Point out that generalizations must be supported by observable facts or statements. Both generalizations above, for example, might be supported by personal observations.

SUMMARIZE Remind students that when they *summarize,* they give just the main points of something they have read. Briefly summarize a story they have read in class and ask students why you didn't include a specific detail or two from the story.

ADDITIONAL SKILL INSTRUCTION

PLOT Review with students that the *plot* of a story is what happens. Have volunteers retell the plot by telling what happened first, in the middle, and at the end of the story *The Winning Point!*

Generalize

- A **generalization** is a broad statement that applies to many examples.

Directions Read the following paragraph.

> Soccer has been played around the world for many years. But it is not as popular in the United States as it is in other countries. It is a game similar to basketball or American football. In each game, two teams of players face each other. They try to get the ball into a goal at the other end of the playing field. They also try to prevent the other team from getting the ball into their goal. Goals score points. The team with the most points wins.

Directions Put a check mark by the generalization you could make about the paragraph.

_____ Soccer is similar to basketball.

_____ Soccer is not as popular here as in other countries.

_____ In soccer, goals score points.

Directions Write a fact that supports the generalization above.

_____

_____

_____

Name _____

Vocabulary

Directions Write the vocabulary word that fits with each group.

Check the Words You Know

___basketball	___disease	___freeze
___guard	___popular	___sports
___study	___terrible	

1. liked by many

common

wanted

_____

2. horrible

very bad

the worst

_____

3. has a high basket

get the ball in

run down the court

_____

4. flu

sickness

fever

_____

5. baseball

soccer

basketball

_____

6. read carefully

think hard

try to learn

_____

7. protect

watch out for

prevent

_____

8. icy

stop cold

can't move

_____

How to Measure the Weather

SUMMARY This nonfiction reader describes aspects of weather—temperature, wind, precipitation, and air pressure—and the tools that meteorologists use to measure these phenomena.

LESSON VOCABULARY

average	depth
desert	erupted
outrun	peak
tides	waterfalls

INTRODUCE THE BOOK

INTRODUCE THE TITLE AND AUTHOR Discuss with students the title and the author of *How to Measure the Weather*. Point out the genre and content triangle and discuss with students what sort of information might be included in the book. Ask: What tools do we use for measuring? (*Possible responses: rulers, scales, measuring cups and spoons, thermometers*)

BUILD BACKGROUND Put the word *weather* at the center of a concept web on the board. Invite students to brainstorm the words and ideas that come to mind when they think of the word *weather*. Review the measuring tools students suggested when talking about the title of the selection. Ask students what measuring tools they think are used to measure weather.

PREVIEW/USE TEXT FEATURES Tell students to skim through the text by looking at the photos. Have students focus on the photos of instruments and point out any that they recognize. Explain that all of the instruments shown are used to measure weather. Then have students predict what some of the unfamiliar instruments measure, based on what is shown in the nearby photographs.

READ THE BOOK

SET PURPOSE Have students set a purpose for reading the selection by completing the following sentence: I want to read this book because I want to find out more about _____. Tell students to fill in the blank with a topic about measuring the weather.

STRATEGY SUPPORT: IMPORTANT IDEAS Tell students that authors have many important ideas in a story. Understanding which ideas are important will help the students better understand the story. Ask students to keep this in mind as they read.

COMPREHENSION QUESTIONS

PAGE 7 What question could you ask about wind that is answered on this page? (*Possible response: What is a wind named after?*)

PAGE 9 What does an anemometer use to measure the speed of wind? (*cups that spin*)

PAGE 11 What is the main idea of this page? (*Possible response: You can make your own rain gauge to measure how much rain has fallen.*)

PAGE 12 What comparison does the author make on this page? (*Thermometers, weather vanes, anemometers, rain gauges, and barometers all measure weather.*)

REVISIT THE BOOK

READER RESPONSE

1. Possible response: The photographs give you a way to see what is being discussed. You can visualize the instruments and the different types of weather described in the selection.
2. Possible response: How to name wind. How to measure rainfall and wind speed.
3. *Waterfalls, yardsticks;* Sentences will vary.
4. The wind is coming from the south. The arrow is pointing to "S."

EXTEND UNDERSTANDING Explain that authors often include photographs in nonfiction books to help readers understand what happens in the text. Discuss with students how the pictures of the weather instruments in this selection helped them better understand the tools and how they work.

RESPONSE OPTIONS

WORD WORK Provide students with the etymology of the word *meteorology*: *meteor-* meaning "things in the air" and *-ology* meaning "the science of." Have students look up the definition of *meteorology* in a dictionary and write a brief paragraph comparing today's definition of the word with its origin.

SCIENCE CONNECTION

Have students create their own weather stations at home that include a thermometer and rain gauge (a simple can or jug to collect water). Tell students to take readings of the thermometer and rain gauges once a day every day for a week and chart their readings in a table. Have students compare tables at the end of the week and plot their readings on classroom graphs.

Skill Work

TEACH/REVIEW VOCABULARY

List the vocabulary words on the board and go over the definitions. Divide the class into groups, and assign each group a vocabulary word. Have each group create clues for its word. Clues may relate to the meaning, spelling, part of speech, or pronunciation of the word. Then have groups give their clues to the class while other students try to guess the word.

ELL Have students work in pairs to illustrate the vocabulary words. Assign the more difficult words, such as *average* and *depth*, to more proficient students.

TARGET SKILL AND STRATEGY

GRAPHIC SOURCES Remind students that *graphic sources* include charts, tables, diagrams, maps, or pictures with captions. Looking at graphic sources can help readers understand information by presenting it visually. Ask students to talk about any graphic source in *How to Measure the Weather* that was particularly helpful to them and tell why.

IMPORTANT IDEAS Remind students that when they read, it helps to find important ideas in the story. Explain that authors can organize the text of a story so important ideas are easier to find. Ask students how the text is organized. *(by description)* Tell students that the descriptions the author gives are some of the important ideas of the story.

ADDITIONAL SKILL INSTRUCTION

MAIN IDEA AND DETAILS Review with students that a *main idea* is the most important idea about a topic. *Supporting details* tell more about the main idea. On the board, list the weather instruments from the selection. Have students choose one instrument to focus on. As students read, have them look for the main idea about their topic. When students have finished reading, tell them to write the main idea in a sentence. Then have them find two supporting details in the book that tell more about this main idea.

Name _____

Graphic Sources

- **Graphic sources** present information visually and can help you better understand the text.
- Graphic sources include charts, tables, diagrams, maps, and pictures with captions.

Directions Study the following graphic source. Then answer the questions below.

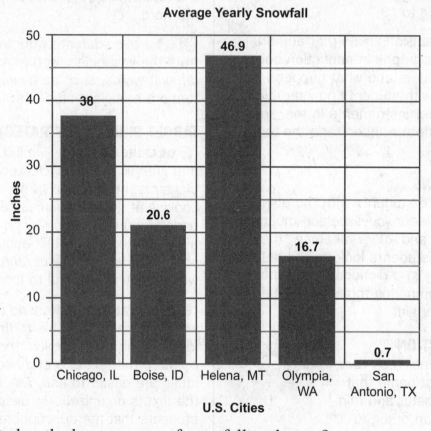

1. Which city has the least amount of snowfall each year?

_____

2. Which city receives the most snowfall each year?

_____

3. Does Chicago have more or less snowfall each year than Helena? than Boise?

_____

4. Why do you think that San Antonio, TX, has such little snowfall?

_____

5. Why do you think that Chicago, IL, has so much snowfall each year?

Name _____

Vocabulary

Directions Draw lines to match the words with their definitions.

Check the Words You Know

___average ___depth ___desert ___erupted
___outrun ___peak ___tides ___waterfalls

1. depth   **a.** the pointed top of a mountain or hill

2. outrun   **b.** the distance from the top to the bottom

3. average   **c.** burst violently

4. peak   **d.** dry, sandy region without water or trees

5. desert   **e.** to run faster than someone or something

6. waterfalls   **f.** the quantity found by dividing the sum of all the quantities by the number of quantities

7. tides   **g.** the rise and fall of the ocean

8. erupted   **h.** streams of water that fall from a high place

Directions Imagine you are an explorer. Write a brief paragraph about one of your adventures using the words *desert, outrun, peak, tides,* and *waterfalls.*

_____

_____

_____

_____

_____

_____

Grandpa's Rock Kit

SUMMARY In *Grandpa's Rock Kit,* a mother teaches her two children everything her father taught her about rocks. The selection describes the three kinds of rocks that make up the Earth's crust and gives examples of each.

LESSON VOCABULARY

attic	board	chores
customers	labeled	spare
stamps		

INTRODUCE THE BOOK

INTRODUCE THE TITLE AND AUTHOR Discuss with students the title and the author of *Grandpa's Rock Kit*. Ask: What does the word *kit* make you think of? (Possible response: a box with materials to make something) What do you think might be inside a rock kit? (Possible response: rocks and other things to help you make something with the rocks) Explain to students that in this story, a *kit* is a collection.

ELL For students unfamiliar with the word *kit*, point out that many words have more than one meaning. Introduce students to the multiple meanings of the word *kit*, and reinforce the Build Background activity by emphasizing the meaning used in this story.

BUILD BACKGROUND Bring in a variety of rocks to share with the class. If possible, include some examples of rocks mentioned in the reader. Pass the rocks around the class and have students describe what they see and feel. Invite volunteers to share what they know about the different types of rocks found on Earth. Write their ideas on the board. Point out that students will read about Earth's variety of rocks in this story.

PREVIEW/USE TEXT FEATURES Have students look through the pictures in the book. Discuss with students what the people in the pictures seem to be doing. Then focus on the rock diagrams and pictures.

READ THE BOOK

SET PURPOSE To guide students in setting their purposes for reading, have them look at the W section of the class KWL chart about rocks. Tell each student to choose one fact they want to know about rocks and use it to complete the following sentence: I want to read this story because I want to know _____.

STRATEGY SUPPORT: INFERRING Explain to students that when they *infer* they combine prior knowledge with information from the text, to learn something new. Inferring will help students make a decision or opinion about what they have read. Ask students to make inferences as they read.

COMPREHENSION QUESTIONS

PAGE 3 Can you find a statement of opinion on this page? Who says it? (*Mom says cleaning out the attic will be fun.*)

PAGES 6–7 Is there anything on this page that you already know something about? How does your knowledge help you understand the information here? (*Possible response: I know that when volcanoes erupt, lava comes out. Since I already know what lava is, I understand better how lava becomes igneous rock.*)

PAGE 9 What is one type of sedimentary rock? How does its name tell you something about its qualities? (*sandstone; it's soft like sand*)

PAGE 11 What generalization can you find on this page? (*Possible response: Marble is usually white.*)

REVISIT THE BOOK

READER RESPONSE

1. Possible response: Heat and pressure change some rocks into metamorphic rocks. Grandpa's rocks are really neat.
2. Responses will vary but should include a combination of prior knowledge and new text.
3. Possible response: The attic in our house is always cold because there is no heat up there.
4. the core

EXTEND UNDERSTANDING

Review with students the KWL chart on the board. Look through all the facts about rocks that students wanted to know. Then fill in what they learned about rocks. Have students tell where they found their facts in the book. Discuss where students might look to find out more about rocks.

RESPONSE OPTIONS

WRITING Have students research different types of rocks. Tell students to create an encyclopedia entry for their rock in which they describe the rock's qualities; tell whether the rock is igneous, sedimentary, or metamorphic; and explain where the rock is usually found. Collect the entries into a classroom rock encyclopedia.

SCIENCE CONNECTION

Have students make categories for the various types of rocks in their rock encyclopedia. Tell students to start by grouping their rocks as either igneous or sedimentary or metamorphic. Then have students come up with other categories for the rocks based on their characteristics or where they are found. Use the category lists as an index for the rock encyclopedia.

Skill Work

TEACH/REVIEW VOCABULARY

Divide students into groups and assign one vocabulary word to each group. Have members of the group find the word's definition in the dictionary; write a sentence for the word; illustrate the word; and share the definition, sentence, and illustration with the class.

TARGET SKILL AND STRATEGY

FACT AND OPINION Tell students that a statement of *fact* can be proved true or false, but a statement of *opinion* is a person's ideas or feelings about a topic. Remind students that they do not actually have to prove a statement of fact true or false, but just be able to decide whether it can be checked. Have students look for statements of facts and opinions in the text as they read.

INFERRING Remind students to think about information they know along with information about the text as they read. Ask students to use this new information to form their own ideas about the text. Tell students to share the new information they have inferred.

ADDITIONAL SKILL INSTRUCTION

CAUSE AND EFFECT Review with students that a *cause* is why something happened and an *effect* is what happened. Tell students that the effect usually follows the cause. Ask students to turn to page 9. Point out that sedimentary rocks are formed *(effect)* by the top layers of sand pressing down on them *(cause)*.

Fact and Opinion

- A statement of **fact** is one that can be proved true or false.
- A statement of **opinion** is someone's judgment, belief, or way of thinking about something.

Directions Write *F* beside statements of fact and *O* beside statements of opinion.

1. _____ Since it was Sunday, Danny and Tina helped their mother with chores.

2. _____ Rock kits contain many different types of rocks.

3. _____ The middle layer of the earth's crust is called the mantle.

4. _____ Although limestone can be found in many different colors, it is the most beautiful rock.

5. _____ Sedimentary rocks are the most common rocks.

6. _____ Fossils can be found in certain rocks.

7. _____ Grandpa's rock collection contained many neat rocks.

8. _____ Limestone, metamorphic rock, and granite can be found in many different colors.

9–10. Directions Read the statement: *Limestone would be more interesting to study than granite.* Is it a fact or an opinion? Why?

_____

_____

_____

_____

_____

Vocabulary

Directions Unscramble each of the following words.

Check the Words You Know

___attic   ___board   ___chores   ___customer
___labeled   ___spare   ___stamps

1. rhesoc _____

2. dellbae _____

3. itcat _____

4. pastsm _____

5. odrab _____

4. reaps _____

5. stromcuse _____

Directions Use four of the words that you unscrambled in a paragraph about something you did on a Saturday afternoon. Your paragraph can tell about something real or imaginary.

_____

_____

_____

_____

Across the English Channel

SUMMARY This nonfiction reader tells about some of the earliest attempts to swim across the English Channel and highlights a few of the cross-channel record holders. The book also describes the conditions in the Channel that make it such a challenging body of water for swimmers.

LESSON VOCABULARY

celebrate	continued
current	drowned
medal	stirred
strokes	

INTRODUCE THE BOOK

INTRODUCE THE TITLE AND AUTHOR Discuss the title and the author of *Across the English Channel*. Ask students to predict what the English Channel is, based on the cover photographs. Discuss with students who the woman pictured on the cover might be.

BUILD BACKGROUND By a show of hands, find out how many students in the class like to swim. Have volunteers talk about where they like to swim, such as in pools, lakes, or the ocean. Tell students to describe what they like most about swimming in these places and what they like the least.

ELL Have students describe their favorite swimming places in their home countries and compare them with places where they have gone swimming in the United States.

PREVIEW/USE TEXT FEATURES Explain to students that the selection is about a body of water called the English Channel. Have students look at the maps on pages 3 and 6. Discuss with students what conditions in the Channel might be like. Then have students skim through the rest of the pictures in the book. Ask students to describe the people in the pictures and what they seem to be doing.

READ THE BOOK

SET PURPOSE Invite students to look at the cover of the reader once again. Help them to set a purpose for reading by having them complete the following statement: "I would like to read this book about the English Channel to find out more about _____."

STRATEGY SUPPORT: QUESTIONING Tell students to see what questions the author raises and how reading further helps you answer them. After reading, encourage students to think about what they read and to go back to the text for answers. As they begin to formulate a generalization, these questions and answers will help them assess the importance of what they read.

COMPREHENSION QUESTIONS

PAGES 6–7 What general statement can you make about the English Channel? *(Possible response: It is always difficult to swim across the English Channel.)*

PAGES 8–9 Is there anything you find confusing on these pages? What fix-up strategy can you use? *(Possible response: I was confused about how Gertrude Ederle broke the men's record by two hours when Matthew Webb swam the Channel in 22 hours. Then I reread and realized that Ederle broke the men's record of her period, not Webb's old record.)*

PAGE 10 Find a statement of fact on this page. How do you know it is a statement of fact? *(Possible response: Others are part of a team of two or more swimmers. It can be proved true or false by checking in a book.)*

PAGE 12 Find a statement of opinion in the first paragraph on this page and tell how you know it is an opinion. *(Possible response: That difficult task seems like something to celebrate. It's an opinion because it's the author's belief about why someone should celebrate.)*

REVISIT THE BOOK

READER RESPONSE

1. Possible responses: Facts: The English Channel is a narrow body of water (p. 3). Many kinds of goods are carried through the Channel each day (p. 4). Opinions: Some swimmers see these wild waters as a challenge (p. 7). That was an awesome feat (p. 9)!

2. Responses will vary but should include a question and show understanding of the text.

3. *Stir* may also mean "to mix." Possible responses: The wind stirred the leaves gently. She stirred the cake batter until it was smooth.

4. Possible response: I would like to run a marathon because that is the ultimate running challenge!

EXTEND UNDERSTANDING Explain to students that *graphic sources* are visual aids, such as maps, graphs, time lines, and pictures with captions, that help the reader understand the text. Point out that sometimes graphics provide additional information. Have students look through the pictures and captions in *Across the English Channel* and find one piece of information that they learned from the captions that was not in the text. Invite volunteers to share their answers.

RESPONSE OPTIONS

WRITING Tell students to think of an amazing feat that they might try, such as swimming underwater the entire length of a pool. Have students write a plan to prepare for their feat, including information on training, diet, and equipment.

SOCIAL STUDIES CONNECTION

Explain to students that a *strait* is a type of channel. Have students research other famous channels and straits from around the globe, including the Bering Strait, the Bosporus Strait, and the Strait of Magellan. Tell students to write brief reports describing the geography and conditions of their channels, as well as how people use them today.

Skill Work

TEACH/REVIEW VOCABULARY

Write a sentence for each word on the chalkboard. Have volunteers guess the meanings of the words by using context clues. Then have other students look up each word in the dictionary and tell the class the definition.

TARGET SKILL AND STRATEGY

FACT AND OPINION Explain to students that a *statement of fact* is a statement that can be proved true or false. A *statement of opinion* is a person's beliefs or ideas about something. Point out that as readers they just need to know that the statement can be checked by looking in reference sources, by asking an expert, or by observing. Give examples of statements of facts and opinions, and discuss with students how to distinguish each. Then tell students to look for at least one statement of fact and one statement of opinion in the reader.

QUESTIONING As students read, have them ask themselves about swimming the English Channel. Help them organize their answers into logical generalizations.

ADDITIONAL SKILL INSTRUCTION

GENERALIZE Explain to students that sometimes authors make a statement about several ideas or things in a book. The statement can tell how the ideas or things are all alike or mostly alike or how they are all or mostly different. Provide examples of generalizations that state how things in a group are alike or different. As students read, have them look for a general statement that the author makes about the English Channel.

Fact and Opinion

- A statement of **fact** is a statement that can be proved true or false. You can check a statement of fact by looking in reference sources, asking an expert, or observing.
- A statement of **opinion** is a person's beliefs or ideas about something. You cannot prove whether it is true or false.

Directions Decide whether each sentence below is a statement of fact or opinion. Write your answer on the line.

1. The English Channel is about 350 miles long.

   _____

2. The English Channel is not very deep.

   _____

3. There is always a chance that a swimmer could drown.

   _____

4. In 1926, Gertrude Ederle of the United States became the first woman to swim across the English Channel.

   _____

5. But if you have the stamina, the skill, and the desire for a challenge, you might consider swimming as an alternate way to cross the English Channel.

   _____

Vocabulary

Directions Fill in each column of the chart below with the correct words from the box
You may use a word more than once.

Check the Words You Know

____celebrate   ____continued   ____current   ____drowned
____medal   ____stirred   ____strokes

Singular Nouns	Verbs in Past Tense	Words with Endings
1.	3.	6.
2.	4.	7.
	5.	8.
		9.

Directions Write an original paragraph about something special that you did. How
did you celebrate? Describe your accomplishment and use the word *celebrate* in your
paragraph.

_____

_____

_____

_____

_____

Swimming Like Buck

SUMMARY This fictional story is a funny retelling of *Swimming Like Buck*. It gives students information about being proud of who they are and puts forth the idea that things that seem to be holding you back can often be a benefit.

LESSON VOCABULARY

clutched	echoed
gully	reeds
scrambled	thatch
valley	

INTRODUCE THE BOOK

INTRODUCE THE TITLE AND AUTHOR Discuss the title and author of the book *Swimming Like Buck* with students. Ask students what the title makes them think the story might be about. Direct students' attention to the cover illustration and discuss what is happening in the picture and how it might relate to the story.

BUILD BACKGROUND Ask students if they have ever been teased for doing something differently than everybody else. Discuss how students handled the teasing, and then suggest why doing things differently can actually be beneficial.

PREVIEW Invite students to look through the illustrations of the story. Ask students if they can get an idea about the story just from looking at the pictures; then ask students how the drawings help them determine if this will be a funny or sad story.

READ THE BOOK

SET PURPOSE Have students set a purpose for reading *Swimming Like Buck*. Students' interest in how to handle teasing and their love of animal stories should help guide this purpose.

STRATEGY SUPPORT: MONITOR AND CLARIFY Explain to students the importance of *monitoring,* or keeping an eye on, their understanding of what they are reading. Remind them that there are different ways to *clarify* a comprehension problem. For example, students can write notes about what is happening and check their notes if the story stops making sense. Students can also read on to clear up any confusion.

COMPREHENSION QUESTIONS

PAGE 3 What was the big problem Buck had to solve in this story? *(He was being teased because of the way he was swimming.)*

PAGE 7 How else do you think Buck could have handled the teasing? *(Possible responses: He did the right thing. He could have kept swimming and ignored them.)*

PAGE 9 What does the coach's opinion tell you about how you see yourself and how others see you? *(Possible response: You should be proud of being different even though others may make fun of you.)*

PAGES 10–11 Using a graphic organizer, list the steps of how Buck and Quack became friends. *(Step 1: Buck joined the team and won every race. Step 2: Buck became famous for his swimming style. Step 3: Quack got Buck's autograph and asked if he could learn Buck's special style. Step 4: Buck said he would teach him.)*

REVISIT THE BOOK

READER RESPONSE

1. Buck swam differently (cause) so other ducks made fun of him (effect). Buck won every race (cause) and made a new friend (effect).

2. Response will vary but should show clarification of confusion.

3. Sentences should reflect understanding of word meaning and of past tense.

4. By forgiving Quack, Buck taught him that kindness is important. Possible response: I would have forgiven Quack.

EXTEND UNDERSTANDING Remind students that the sequence of events is the order in which things happen in a story. Ask students to make a time line of all the events that happen to Buck, and then discuss how one event leads to another and then finally to the happy ending.

RESPONSE OPTIONS

WRITING Suggest students imagine they are Quack, and have them write an apology to Buck.

LITERATURE CONNECTION

Have students reread *The Ugly Duckling* and then ask them to compare the story with *Swimming Like Buck*.

Skill Work

TEACH/REVIEW VOCABULARY

Hide definitions for the vocabulary words around the classroom near, on, or under things that start with the same letter as the vocabulary word—for example the definition for *scrambled* could be hidden by the sharpener. Tell students each word, and then have them look for its definition.

ELL Have students write the definition of each vocabulary word on one side of a card and the word on the other. They can use the cards to test themselves or other students.

TARGET SKILL AND STRATEGY

CAUSE AND EFFECT Remind students that usually there is a reason (cause) why something happens (effect) in a story. Point out that often what happens *follows* why the event happened. Direct students to look for what happens to Buck and why.

MONITOR AND CLARIFY Tell students that they should *monitor* their understanding of a story as they read. Tell them that when a story stops making sense, there are things they can do to *clarify* any problems they have with understanding. Model using page 7. Say: The ducks call Buck an alligator. This is confusing. I thought Buck was a duck! I read on and found out the other ducks thought Buck looked like an alligator when he swam. Remind students if they clarify any comprehension problems they might have, they will better understand what they read.

ADDITIONAL SKILL INSTRUCTION

CHARACTER Remind students that a character is the person or animal who does the action or talking in the book. Invite students to draw a character map of Buck, with the headings "What Buck Thinks of Himself," "What Others Think or Say About Buck," and "What Buck Does." Suggest that as students read the book, they fill in information from the story under each heading.

Name _____

Cause and Effect

- A **cause** is why something happened. An **effect** is what happened. Look for clue words.

Directions Use the story *Swimming Like Buck* to complete the chart below. For each event that happened in the story, fill in why the event happened.

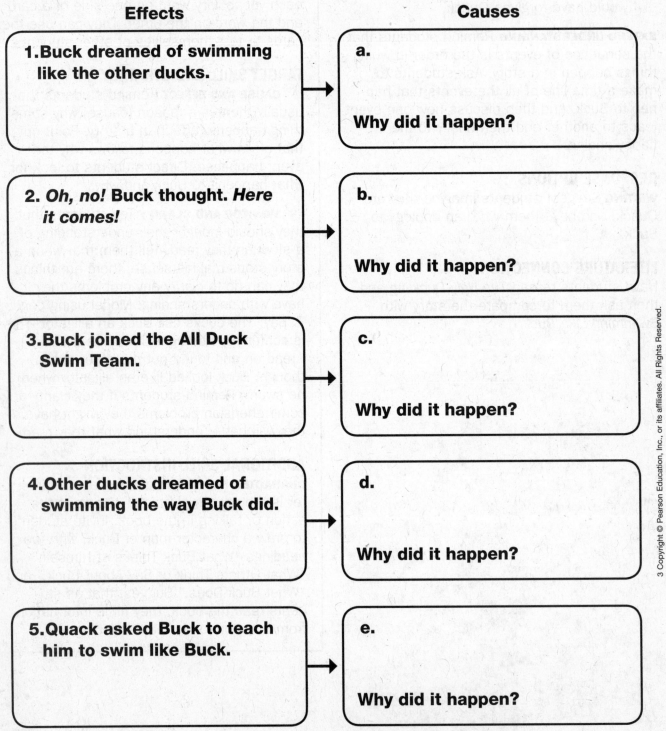

Effects	Causes
1. Buck dreamed of swimming like the other ducks.	a. Why did it happen?
2. *Oh, no!* Buck thought. *Here it comes!*	b. Why did it happen?
3. Buck joined the All Duck Swim Team.	c. Why did it happen?
4. Other ducks dreamed of swimming the way Buck did.	d. Why did it happen?
5. Quack asked Buck to teach him to swim like Buck.	e. Why did it happen?

Vocabulary

Directions Write the definition of each word in the space provided.

Check the Words You Know

___clutched   ___echoed   ___gully   ___reeds

___scrambled   ___thatch   ___valley

1. clutched

_____

2. echoed

_____

3. gully

_____

4. reeds

_____

5. scrambled

_____

6. valley

_____

7. thatch

_____

Directions Write two sentences about Buck using two words from the word box.

8. _____

_____

9. _____

A Tea Party with Obâchan

SUMMARY This story tells about Anna and the Japanese culture of her mother and grandmother. Anna joins her grandmother for tea and learns more about her Japanese heritage.

LESSON VOCABULARY

cotton	festival
graceful	handkerchief
paces	pale
rhythm	snug

INTRODUCE THE BOOK

INTRODUCE THE TITLE AND AUTHOR Discuss with the students the title and the author of the selection *A Tea Party with Obâchan*. Ask students what they know about the items on the cover.

BUILD BACKGROUND Discuss with students what they know about Japan and Japanese culture. Ask them to discuss what they know about Japanese culture, including food, language, and traditional clothing.

PREVIEW/USE ILLUSTRATIONS Invite students to look at the illustrations in the book. Ask students if anything in the illustrations is familiar to them, and if not, what in each illustration looks interesting to them.

READ THE BOOK

SET PURPOSE Have students set a purpose for reading *A Tea Party with Obâchan*. Students' curiosity about Japan and other foreign cultures should guide this purpose.

STRATEGY SUPPORT: VISUALIZE Ask students to visualize or form pictures in their minds to better understand the information in the book as they read. Read page 9 and then ask students to close their eyes while you reread the page. Encourage students to use prior knowledge to help form pictures in their minds. Ask students to share what pictures they saw in their minds as you read.

COMPREHENSION QUESTIONS

PAGE 3 What clothing does Anna wear to have tea with her Obâchan? *(a kimono)*

PAGES 6–7 How does Anna show that she is curious about the Japanese culture? *(Possible response: She asks her grandma questions about the things she sees while visiting for tea. She wants to go to Japan.)*

PAGES 8–11 What do you like about Japanese culture? *(Possible responses: I like the kimonos. I like the drum or taiko. I like the Flower Festival.)*

REVISIT THE BOOK

READER RESPONSE

1. Responses will vary but should include information from the text.
2. Possible response: I pictured Obâchan walking gracefully which helped me understand that learning about a culture takes time.
3. light
4. Possible response: She wanted to learn more about her culture and see all of the things that her grandma spoke about.

EXTEND UNDERSTANDING Students may want to put themselves in Anna's place. Help students see that authors often write characters so that the reader can identify with them or want to be like them. Ask students what made the character of Anna believable. Their responses may help them with writing in response to the story.

RESPONSE OPTIONS

WRITING Ask students to write a letter to an imaginary pen pal in Japan. Discuss with students the kinds of questions they might have for their pen pal and the kinds of questions they imagine their pen pal might have for them. Encourage students to include drawings about the United States or pictures they can cut out of old magazines.

SOCIAL STUDIES CONNECTION

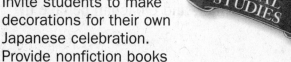

Invite students to make decorations for their own Japanese celebration. Provide nonfiction books that depict celebrations such as the Japanese New Year, Coming of Age Day, or the Flower Festival. From their research or the story, have them create decorations in a way that reflects the celebration.

Skill Work

TEACH/REVIEW VOCABULARY

Review vocabulary words with students. Then, for the word *cotton*, ask students, "If you were wearing something made of cotton, what would it feel like?" Personalize all other vocabulary words in this same way.

ELL Go over vocabulary words with students. Then have them suggest a sentence for each word.

TARGET SKILL AND STRATEGY

COMPARE AND CONTRAST Explain to students that when we *compare* and *contrast,* we describe how two things are alike and different. Tell students that clue words, such as *like, similarly,* or *in contrast,* are not always present, and readers must decide for themselves when comparisons or contrasts are being made. As they read, have students look for one example of a comparison or a contrast in the text.

VISUALIZE After students finish reading, ask them to think about the most interesting part of the story. Ask students to close their eyes and make pictures in their minds about the things they found interesting. Tell students to describe the pictures they formed. Ask: How does the picture in your mind help you remember more of the details from the story?

ADDITIONAL SKILL INSTRUCTION

GENERALIZE Remind students that a *generalization* is a broad statement or rule that applies to many examples and is made after thinking about what the facts have in common. Generalizations often have clue words such as *everyone, many, always, usually, seldom,* and *in general.* Remind them that not all generalizations are valid. Examples: "All animals with fur hibernate" or "All robins fly." Discuss whether these generalizations are valid. As students read, ask them to write two valid generalizations.

Compare and Contrast

- When you **compare** two or more things, you think about how they are alike and how they are different.
- When you **contrast** two of more things, you only think about how they are different.

Directions Reread the story *A Tea Party with Obâchan*. Then use the chart below to fill in the facts about Anna, Anna's mother, and Obâchan's characteristics.

Anna	Anna's Mother	Obâchan
1. _____	3. _____	5. _____
2. _____	4. _____	6. _____

7. Write a general statement about how Anna, Anna's mother, and Obâchan behave in similar ways.

_____

_____

8. Write a general statement about how the characters behave in different ways.

_____

_____

Vocabulary

Directions On Japanese New Year, families play a game called Karula. Parts of poems are printed on cards. Players match the cards to read the poems out loud. Using the vocabulary words, make up a poem. Then write out the definitions of each word.

Check the Words You Know

___cotton   ___festival   ___graceful   ___handkerchief
___paces   ___pale   ___rhythm   ___snug

Your Poem

_____

_____

_____

_____

_____

_____

_____

Your Definitions

cotton _____

festival _____

graceful _____

handkerchief _____

paces _____

pale _____

rhythm _____

snug _____

Celebrate Independence Day Celebrar el Día de la Independencia

SUMMARY This reader discusses how America and Mexico both gained their independence. The selection gives students a look at the ways that Americans and Mexicans celebrate their freedom.

LESSON VOCABULARY

bouquets	circus
difficult	nibble
piers	soar
swallow	

INTRODUCE THE BOOK

INTRODUCE THE TITLE AND AUTHOR Discuss with students the title and the author of *Celebrate Independence Day, Celebrar el Día de la Independencia*. Based on the title, ask students what kind of information they think this book will provide. Have students look at the cover photographs to see if they can get additional clues about the book's content.

BUILD BACKGROUND Discuss with students what they know about America's desire to become independent. Ask students what they do to celebrate Independence Day.

PREVIEW/USE TEXT FEATURES Invite students to look at the illustrations and captions in the book. Ask students how these text features give clues about what is going to be discussed in the text.

READ THE BOOK

SET PURPOSE Have students set a purpose for reading *Celebrate Independence Day, Celebrar el Día de la Independencia.* Students may want to focus on how America and Mexico became independent.

STRATEGY SUPPORT: INFERRING Remind students that when they *infer* they combine prior knowledge to help them create their own ideas about the text. Ask students: Why did America want to become a free country? *(They were not happy under the king of England's rule.)*

COMPREHENSION QUESTIONS

PAGE 4 Why did the colonists in America want to be independent? *(They wanted to make their own laws and government.)*

PAGE 9 Identify one fact from page 9. *(Possible responses: The people of Mexico fought in a war that lasted eleven years. They won their freedom from Spain. Mexico celebrates Independence Day on September 16. Independence Day in Spanish is* el Día de la Independencia.*)*

PAGE 12 In what ways do you celebrate Independence Day or *el Día de la Independencia? (Responses will vary.)*

REVISIT THE BOOK

READER RESPONSE

1. Responses will vary but should show an understanding of a main idea and includes details.

2. Responses will vary but should include ideas about other celebrations.

3. into the dark night sky

4. Possible responses: Both—People celebrate the freedom of their country from foreign rulers. They celebrate with parades, parties, and fireworks.
Different—United States: People eat hot dogs. Mexico: The President of Mexico rings the bell in Dolores, Mexico.

EXTEND UNDERSTANDING Remind students that a *cause* is why something happened and an *effect* is what happened. Ask students to write down the causes for the United States wanting to be independent, and then in a separate column, write down the effects.

RESPONSE OPTIONS

WRITING Have students imagine that they have just arrived in Mexico. Have them write a letter to a friend in the United States describing what it is like to celebrate *el Día de la Independencia.*

SOCIAL STUDIES CONNECTION

Have students research other countries that gained their independence. Have them find out the reasons that these countries wanted to be independent and how they now celebrate their independence.

Skill Work

TEACH/REVIEW VOCABULARY

Review the vocabulary words. Then play Vocabulary Master with students. Give students three different definitions for each vocabulary word, including one that is silly. Have them select the correct definition and then use the word in a sentence.

ELL Ask students to look through the book and write down any unfamiliar words they come across. Suggest that they look up the words in the dictionary and write the meanings in their notebooks.

TARGET SKILL AND STRATEGY

MAIN IDEA AND DETAILS Tell students that the *main idea* is the most important idea about a topic and the *details* are small pieces of information that tell more about the topic. Model a way of determining the main idea and details of this book by asking: What is this book about in a few words? *(Independence Day)* What is the most important idea of this topic? *(American and Mexican people fought hard for their independence.)*

INFERRING After reading, invite students to think about the information they read. Tell them to create new information using what they read and what they already know. Ask students to share their ideas about the text.

ADDITIONAL SKILL INSTRUCTION

DRAW CONCLUSIONS Remind students that *drawing conclusions* means making a decision that makes sense after thinking about some facts or details. Give students a few sentences about a topic related to this book, and have them draw reasonable conclusions about this topic.

Main Ideas and Details

- The **main idea** is the most important idea about a topic.
- The **details** are the small pieces of information that tell more about the topic.

Directions Read the following passages from *Celebrate Independence Day, Celebrar el Día de la Independencia.* Circle the correct main idea in each.

1. The Declaration of Independence stated the thirteen colonies wanted to separate from Great Britain. A difficult war with Great Britain followed. Finally, independence from Great Britain was won.
   a. The War was difficult against Great Britain.
   b. Independence was gained from Great Britain.
   c. The thirteen colonies wanted to separate from Great Britain.

2. On the eve of *el Día de la Independencia* the President of Mexico rings the same bell that rang in Dolores in 1810. He then gives the *Grito de Dolores* speech again. Then the celebration begins!
   a. The bell from Dolores is rung.
   b. The celebration of *el Día de la Independencia* begins.
   c. The same traditions have been followed for many years.

3. In the United States, people celebrate Independence Day. In Mexico, they celebrate *el Día de la Independencia.* In both places, people celebrate the freedom of their country from foreign rule.
   a. People celebrate the freedom of their country from foreign rule.
   b. National celebrations in the United States and Mexico are wonderful.
   c. Independence Day can be said in many languages.

Directions Look at the main ideas below. Think of a supporting detail for each idea. For example, if the main idea is "Neil loves football," a supporting detail might be "He plays it every Saturday."

4. Doing your homework is important. _____

_____

5. My dad loves the beach. _____

_____

Name _____

Vocabulary

Directions Read each sentence. Write the word from the word box that best matches the definition.

Check the Words You Know

___bouquets   ___circus   ___difficult   ___nibble
___piers   ___soar   ___swallow

_____ **1.** *adj.* hard to do or understand

_____ **2.** *v.* to fly upward

_____ **3.** *n.* bunches of flowers

_____ **4.** *n.* a traveling show of performers

_____ **5.** *n.* docks built over water

_____ **6.** *v.* to take into the stomach through the throat

_____ **7.** *v.* to eat in small bites

Directions Write a paragraph discussing the celebrations described in *Celebrate Independence Day, Celebrar el Día de la Independencia,* using as many vocabulary words as possible.

_____

_____

_____

_____

_____

_____

_____

A Child's Life in Korea

SUMMARY A child's life in Korea is similar in many ways to a child's life in the United States. On the other hand, there are also differences. Korean customs, school life, and holidays are all described in this book.

LESSON VOCABULARY

airport	curious
delicious	described
farewell	homesick
memories	raindrops

INTRODUCE THE BOOK

INTRODUCE THE TITLE AND AUTHOR Discuss with students the title and the author of *A Child's Life in Korea*. Ask students to discuss what they think the book will be about based on the title and the cover illustration. Ask whether the social studies content triangle suggests that this is a work of fiction or nonfiction.

BUILD BACKGROUND Invite students to talk about friends who live in other parts of the world. Ask students how their friends' schools are different from or similar to their own school. Ask students about customs in different parts of the world. Ask: What are some holidays that people in other parts of the world celebrate? How are they like or unlike the holidays we celebrate?

PREVIEW Have students preview the book by looking at the illustrations. Ask them to discuss how these text features give an idea of what this book will cover. Ask what they think they will learn from this book.

READ THE BOOK

SET PURPOSE Have students set a purpose for reading *A Child's Life in Korea*. Students' interest in what schools, holidays, and customs are like in other parts of the world should guide this purpose.

STRATEGY SUPPORT: MONITOR AND FIX UP Invite students to use these fix-up strategies if they find they do not understand something in the text. Encourage them to look back for information they have forgotten. Encourage them to read on to see if basic ideas are explained on the next pages. Challenge them to summarize facts and details after they finish reading.

COMPREHENSION QUESTIONS

PAGE 5 How are the lives of children in South Korea and the United States alike? *(They have families, go to school, and celebrate holidays.)*

PAGE 6 What happens every Monday morning in a South Korean school? *(Students gather outside for the morning meeting.)*

PAGE 9 What is a traditional Saturday activity in Korea? *(visiting grandparents)*

PAGE 10 What do Korean students write about in their journals? *(what happens in their lives at school and at home)*

PAGE 11 What is a Korean custom regarding shoes? *("Outside shoes" are left at the door when entering.)*

PAGE 13 According to a Korean tale, what happens if people fall asleep before midnight on Korean New Year? *(Their eyebrows turn white.)*

REVISIT THE BOOK

READER RESPONSE

1. 1) They gather outside the school. 2) The principal talks about doing well. 3) Prizes are given out. 4) Students take off their shoes and enter the school.
2. Possible response: Family is very important to Koreans. Many holidays involve gathering with family members and showing respect to the oldest members.
3. Responses will vary.
4. Responses will vary.

EXTEND UNDERSTANDING Have students comment on the illustrations in the selection. What details about life in Korea can they learn from the illustrations? Invite them to look at the map on page 4. What information can they learn from the map?

RESPONSE OPTIONS

WRITING Invite students to write one paragraph about their favorite holiday. Challenge them to write the sequence of events that happens on that day.

SOCIAL STUDIES CONNECTION

Time For SOCIAL STUDIES

Students can learn more about life in South Korea by going to the library or using the Internet. Have them find out more about South Korean customs and culture. Ask: What are some favorite foods of South Koreans? What are their favorite sports? What is their capital city? Invite them to share their findings with the class.

Skill Work

TEACH/REVIEW VOCABULARY

Invite students to look up each of the vocabulary words and find out how each word is divided into syllables. Invite them to identify the words that are compounds. (raindrops, farewell, airport, homesick)

ELL Write each of the vocabulary words on an index card. Invite students to take turns choosing a card and acting out something to help others guess the word. Continue until all students have had a chance to act for each word.

TARGET SKILL AND STRATEGY

SEQUENCE Remind students that *sequence* is the order of events—what happens first, next, and last. Explain that clue words such as *first, next,* and *last* are not always present. Invite students to look for information from the book that they can arrange in order. Invite them to add clue words to the events to make the sequence clear.

MONITOR AND FIX UP Remind students that good readers check often to make sure they understand what they read. They also recognize when they have stopped understanding and know some fix-up strategies to restore understanding. Challenge students to ask themselves basic questions as they read: What is the author trying to tell readers? What does this mean? Does this make sense? Explain that tracking the sequence of information in the book can help them better understand what they are reading.

ADDITIONAL SKILL INSTRUCTION

AUTHOR'S PURPOSE Remind students that the author's *purpose* is the reason or reasons an author has for writing. Four common purposes are to persuade, to inform, to entertain, and to express. If an author wants to explain some important information, you may want to read more slowly. Challenge students to determine the author's purpose and adjust the way they read accordingly.

Sequence

- **Sequence** is the order of events in a story.
- Authors sometimes use clue words such as **first, next, then,** and **last** to tell the order of events.

Directions Read the following paragraph based on *A Child's Life in Korea*. Then put the following events in sequence. Write the letters on the lines below.

In South Korea, every Monday morning students gather outside for the morning meeting. First the principal talks to the students to encourage them to do well. Next, prizes are awarded to students for good work. Then children take off their outside shoes and put on special shoes they wear only in the classroom. Finally, they go into the classroom to start their day.

a. The children go inside the classroom.

b. Children take off their outside shoes and put on their special shoes.

c. The principal talks to the students.

d. The children gather for the morning meeting.

e. Prizes are awarded to students for good work.

1. _____

2. _____

3. _____

4. _____

5. _____

Vocabulary

Directions Match the word parts to make compound words. Draw a line from each word beginning to its ending.

Check the Words You Know

___airport   ___curious   ___delicious   ___described
___farewell   ___homesick   ___memories   ___raindrops

1. home   drops

2. fare   sick

3. rain   port

4. air   well

Directions Read each sentence. Write the word from the word box that best completes each sentence.

5. In the book, the author _____ how Koreans celebrate *Solnal,* or Korean New Year.

6. On New Year's Eve, children try to stay awake until after midnight to say

_____ to the past year.

7. Wearing traditional Korean clothing brings back _____ of the past.

8. _____ children can read about Korean customs in books.

9. *Chusok* is a two-day harvest festival when Koreans eat much _____ food.

10. Have you ever felt _____ when you were far away from home?

The World of Bread!

SUMMARY This book is all about bread. The author describes the different types of bread that are made in countries across the globe. The author also discusses the history of bread, how bread is made, and how pizza was invented in Italy.

LESSON VOCABULARY

bakery	batch
boils	braided
dough	ingredients
mixture	

INTRODUCE THE BOOK

INTRODUCE THE TITLE AND AUTHOR Discuss with students the title and author of *The World of Bread!* Based on the book's title, ask students what kind of information they think this book will provide.

BUILD BACKGROUND Ask students to name as many different kinds of bread as they can think of. Ask them if they have ever made or helped make bread. What was the process? What is their favorite kind of bread? What would the world be like without bread?

PREVIEW/SIDEBARS Have students read all the sidebars in the story. What kinds of information are usually given in sidebars?

ELL Have students describe the type of bread made in their native country. What is the word for *bread* in their native language?

READ THE BOOK

SET PURPOSE Have students set a purpose for reading *The World of Bread!* Have them think about the different kinds of bread they have eaten. Suggest that they take notes as they read on the types of bread that were new to them.

STRATEGY SUPPORT: SUMMARIZE Remind students that in order to draw conclusions accurately, good readers check their understanding of what they read. A good way to do this is to summarize a section, or a whole book. For an article, such as *The World of Bread!*, students should be able to tell the main idea and important details. Suggest rereading parts if students don't understand terms or a section's meaning. Students also may use information from the photographs to help them organize their ideas into a summary.

COMPREHENSION QUESTIONS

PAGE 4 What is unusual about the process of making a bagel? *(It is first boiled, and then it is baked.)*

PAGES 5–6 What do the tortilla and chapati have in common? *(Both are round and flat.)*

PAGE 7 Why is pita bread also called "pocket bread"? *(When cut in half, it forms a pocket that can be filled.)*

PAGE 8 What is the smallest grain in the world? Where is it used to make bread? *(teff, comes from Ethiopia)*

PAGE 9 What is special about challah? *(It is eaten by Jewish people on the Sabbath or holidays; it is braided.)*

PAGE 10 Summarize the story of how pizza was invented. *(A baker in Italy made it as a treat for the queen. He made it on flat bread with the colors of the Italian flag: tomatoes (red), cheese (white), and basil (green).)*

REVISIT THE BOOK

READER RESPONSE

1. It is an important food around the world.
2. Possible response: tortilla, chapati, pita, challah
3. flour, water, dough, poppy seeds, sesame seeds
4. People have been making bread for thousands of years.

EXTEND UNDERSTANDING Have students research how flour is produced. They can use the Internet or library resources to gather information. Is flour produced differently in different countries? Is flour always made out of wheat? How was wheat harvested before harvesting machines were invented?

RESPONSE OPTIONS

WRITING Suggest that students write about a memory they have of making bread, watching a family member make bread, or eating freshly baked bread. Have them describe the sights, tastes, and smells. Or have them describe a memory of a trip to a bakery.

SCIENCE CONNECTIONS

Have students research yeast either on the Internet or in the library. How does yeast make bread rise? What kinds of bread is it possible to make without using yeast? How is yeast produced? When did people start making bread with yeast?

Skill Work

TEACH/REVIEW VOCABULARY

To reinforce the contextual meaning of the word *knead* on page 3, discuss how the phrase "and shapes it into a batch of loaves" gives a clue about the meaning. Do the same exercise for the other vocabulary words.

ELL Write each of the vocabulary words on an index card. Invite students to take turns choosing a card and acting out something to help others guess the word. Continue until all students have had a chance to act for each word.

TARGET SKILL AND STRATEGY

DRAW CONCLUSIONS Remind students that *drawing conclusions* means making a decision that makes sense after thinking about facts or details. Have students think about the following question while they read to see if they can draw any conclusions from the text to answer it: Why are there so many different types of bread in the United States?

SUMMARIZE Remind students that *summarizing* is boiling down a story to its main points. Ask students to summarize a familiar story, such as *Jack and the Beanstalk,* or a familiar movie, such as *Finding Nemo.*

ADDITIONAL SKILL INSTRUCTION

MAIN IDEA Remind students that every story has one or more main ideas. Ask students to take notes as they read, listing the main points and supporting details. Ask students to think about what the main idea of this book is.

Draw Conclusions

- To draw a **conclusion** is to think about facts and details and decide something about them.

Directions Read the following passage about chapati. Insert one fact about chapati in each fact box, and then see what conclusion you can draw.

In India, children eat *chapati*. This is a flat, round, chewy bread. The dough is shaped into a circle and browned on both sides in a very hot frying pan. Then it is | held above an open flame for less than a second. This causes the chapati to puff up with steam, like a balloon.

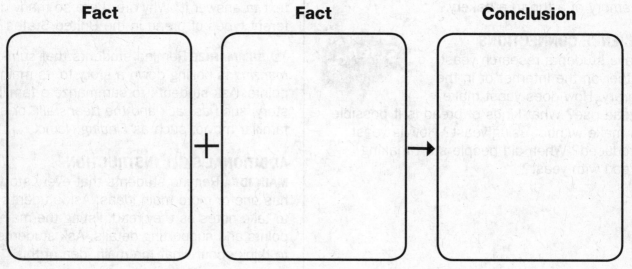

Fact   **Fact**   **Conclusion**

Name _____

Vocabulary

Directions Complete each sentence with the word from the word box that fits best.

<table>
<tr><td colspan="4">**Check the Words You Know**</td></tr>
<tr><td>___bakery</td><td>___batch</td><td>___boils</td><td>___braided</td></tr>
<tr><td>___dough</td><td>___ingredients</td><td>___mixture</td><td></td></tr>
</table>

1. Challah, which is eaten in many Jewish homes on the Sabbath, is often

    _____.

2. To make bread, you have to get the right _____ of flour and water.

3. Before baking bagels, the baker first _____ them.

4. Only the baker knew the proper _____ to make his famous brownies.

5. During Christmas week, the baker always made an extra _____ of Santa Claus cookies.

6. We buy our bread and rolls from a _____.

7. One has to be patient while the _____ is rising.

Directions Write a paragraph about different kinds of bread, using as many vocabulary words as possible.

_____

_____

_____

_____

_____

A Walk Around the City

SUMMARY This nonfiction book shows the many ways people live, work, and play in a city. It focuses on New York City, but it also encourages students to think about their own city and its inhabitants.

LESSON VOCABULARY

cardboard	feast
fierce	flights
pitcher	ruined
stoops	treasure

INTRODUCE THE BOOK

INTRODUCE THE TITLE AND AUTHOR Discuss with students the title and author of *A Walk Around the City*. Ask students what kind of information they think this book will provide based on its title. Ask students to tell whether the scene pictured in the cover photograph is of a small town or a big city. Ask them what clues they used to guess that it's a big city.

BUILD BACKGROUND Discuss with students the various activities in a city. Ask them if they have visited a city other than their own. Ask what they remember about it and the people living there. Ask what they know about cities from television shows, movies, or other books.

PREVIEW/USE TEXT FEATURES Suggest that students skim the heads, photos, and captions in the book. Ask students what clues they used to know this book is about modern-day cities, not those from a century ago.

ELL Ask students to talk about where they used to live. Have them name one difference and one similarity between the place he or she described and the city in the cover photo.

READ THE BOOK

SET PURPOSE Have students set a purpose for reading *A Walk Around the City*. Ask students if they are curious to know about places other than their own city or town. Suggest that they write down notes as they read about any differences between their location and New York City.

STRATEGY SUPPORT: PRIOR KNOWLEDGE Remind students that all cities have some things in common. Suggest that as they read, they think about any personal experiences they have had in a city that are like those discussed in the book. They can also draw on what they have read, heard, or seen about city life. Discuss how using prior knowledge helps readers better understand the author's purpose.

COMPREHENSION QUESTIONS

PAGE 4 Why do you think the author chose to write about New York City? *(She lives there.)*

PAGE 6 Name three ways people use to get around in a city. *(walking, cars, trains, buses, subway)*

PAGE 10 What are two generalizations about cities on this page? Which two words are clue words? *(All cities offer things for people to do for fun. Usually, near the center of a city, you can find museums, zoos, and parks. The clue words are* all *and* usually.*)*

PAGE 12 Can you name another word that means the same thing as *fierce*? Can you think of anything else that you would describe as fierce? *(Possible responses: tough, strong, mean. Tigers and hurricanes can be fierce.)*

REVISIT THE BOOK

READER RESPONSE

1. to inform readers about life in a city
2. Possible responses: Knew: different kinds of buildings, museums; Learned: different city employees, different kinds of commerce
3. the context clue *business*
4. Possible response: The heads are main ideas about the book's topic (cities).

EXTEND UNDERSTANDING Ask students if they have a favorite photograph in the book. Then ask them how the photographs helped them understand the book better. Remind students that captions give more information about the photographs, and can contain details not included in the main text.

RESPONSE OPTIONS

WRITING Ask students to write a paragraph about a trip to a zoo, park, or museum. Suggest that they mention how they got there and why it was fun.

SOCIAL STUDIES CONNECTION

Have students use the library or Internet to find out three details about a city they would like to visit someday. Suggest that they include the population of the city in their notes.

Skill Work

TEACH/REVIEW VOCABULARY

Review the vocabulary words by asking students to define them verbally. Then ask students to use each word in a sentence.

TARGET SKILL AND STRATEGY

AUTHOR'S PURPOSE Remind students that the *author's purpose* is the reason why a writer wrote a particular work. The author's purpose can be to entertain, to persuade, to inform, or to express a mood or feeling. Invite students to discuss why the author wrote *A Walk Around the City*. Then ask students what information they think the author wanted them to learn.

PRIOR KNOWLEDGE Remind students that *prior knowledge* gathered from other books or their personal experiences can help them understand a book and why the author wrote the book. Invite students to create a KWL chart that contains one column each for "What I <u>K</u>now," "What I <u>W</u>ant to Know," and "What I <u>L</u>earned." Prior to reading the book, but after they skim it, ask them to fill in the first and second columns with what they know about cities and what they want to learn. Ask them to fill in the last column after reading the book. Invite students to share their charts with the class.

ADDITIONAL SKILL INSTRUCTION

GENERALIZE Remind students that a *generalization* is a broad statement that applies to many examples. Generalizations often include words such as *many*, *most*, and *generally*. Ask students to use one of these words to write one generalization about what people can do in a city.

Author's Purpose

- The **author's purpose** is the reason or reasons an author has for writing a story.
- An author may have one or more reasons for writing.

Directions Read the following passage. Then answer the questions below.

> Take a walk around your city. You will see people working in bakeries and in all kinds of stores. Walk past a school and see teachers and librarians at work. See the hospital? Nurses and doctors work there. People work at all kinds of jobs in the city.

1. Why do you think the author wrote this passage?

_____

_____

2. What is another reason the author may have written this passage?

_____

_____

3. Why do you think the author asks the reader to "Take a walk around your city"?

_____

_____

4. Why do you think the author mentions teachers, librarians, doctors, and nurses?

_____

_____

Vocabulary

Directions Fill in each blank with the word from the word box that fits best.

Check the Words You Know

___cardboard   ___feast   ___fierce   ___flights

___pitcher   ___ruined   ___stoops   ___treasure

1. When we sat down to lunch, the waiter brought us a _____ of water.

2. The delivery came in a huge _____ box that we used afterwards to build a fort.

3. The highlight of the street fair was a _____ of many different types of food.

4. _____ winds tore the roof off the town hall.

5. A city's most valuable _____ is its people.

6. When the rain came, it _____ our chalk drawings on the sidewalk.

7. Our apartment is up three _____ of stairs.

Directions Write a paragraph about city life that uses several of the vocabulary words.

_____

_____

_____

_____

SUMMARY This book is about the origins of the Statue of Liberty. It also gives students information about Paris and New York around that time and shows how the countries were friends. Students will also learn how the Statue of Liberty became a symbol for freedom for our society.

LESSON VOCABULARY

crown	liberty
models	symbol
tablet	torch
unforgettable	unveiled

INTRODUCE THE BOOK

INTRODUCE THE TITLE AND AUTHOR Discuss with students the title and the author of *The Statue of Liberty: A Gift from France*. Ask students if the title and the photograph on the cover give them any clues as to what this selection is about.

BUILD BACKGROUND Ask students what they know about the Statue of Liberty and if they have ever been to the Statue of Liberty or seen pictures about it. Discuss with students what freedom means to them.

ELL Invite students to talk about important statues in their native countries. Suggest they bring in photographs if they have them, or draw a picture of one of the statues.

PREVIEW/USE TEXT FEATURES Invite students to look at the photographs, captions, and labels in this book. Discuss how each of these text elements gives students a glimpse into what life must have been like in the 1880s in Paris and New York.

READ THE BOOK

SET PURPOSE Have students set a purpose for reading *The Statue of Liberty: A Gift from France*. Students' curiosity about great monuments or about Paris or New York should guide this purpose, but the photographs from the 1800s should also prove fascinating.

STRATEGY SUPPORT: QUESTIONING Explain to students that asking questions involves knowing how to ask good questions about important text information. Create a dialogue where students and you take turns asking questions about the text. Read a section of text together. Model how to ask important questions about it, and call on students to answer the questions. Guide them as they develop their own questions (to be answered by classmates), and encourage them to take over more and more of the activity until they can work independently.

COMPREHENSION QUESTIONS

PAGE 3 What two things did the Statue of Liberty symbolize? *(friendship between France and the United States; freedom)*

PAGE 4 What does the map on page 4 tell you about the city of Paris? *(Possible responses: many roads; the river Seine runs through center of Paris; busy and crowded; a right bank and a left bank)*

PAGE 6 Why do you think Bartholdi made models of every part of the Statue of Liberty before he built it? *(Possible response: Building a small model can save time by giving an idea of what it will look like when large.)*

PAGE 9 What is the main idea on this page? *(New York in the 1880s was full of amazing sights, including the Brooklyn Bridge.)*

PAGE 10 What two text features show you two sides of New York in the 1880s? *(A photograph of immigrants crowded in the city and a photo of a mansion show New York with poor and rich people.)*

REVISIT THE BOOK

READER RESPONSE

1. Responses will vary but should show an understanding of the difference between a fact and an opinion.
2. Responses will vary but should contain a question related to the text and an answer.
3. *Unforgettable*: not able to forget. *Forgettable*: able to be forgotten. *Unpacked*: took out of a crate, box, or case. *Packed*: put into a crate, box, or case. *Unveiled*: took off a covering. *Veiled*: covered.
4. Responses will vary but should contain a statement of opinion.

EXTEND UNDERSTANDING Discuss with students how descriptive words can help you visualize and so better understand what you are reading. Invite students to make a graphic organizer with the headings *Paris* and *New York*. Suggest that students list all the word pictures of Paris and of New York that they find in this book, and that they can also add any descriptive words of their own into this organizer.

RESPONSE OPTIONS

WRITING Suggest students imagine that they are the Statue of Liberty and have them write about what it was like to look at New York City from your island in New York Harbor.

SOCIAL STUDIES CONNECTION

Suggest students do more research on why the Statue of Liberty is a symbol of freedom. Invite students to make up and draw their own symbols of freedom. Post around the classroom.

Time For SOCIAL STUDIES

Skill Work

TEACH/REVIEW VOCABULARY

Review vocabulary words with students. Then, write down a list of definitions in one row and the list of vocabulary words in another and have students match the words to the correct definitions.

TARGET SKILL AND STRATEGY

FACT AND OPINION Share with students that a statement of *fact* is something that can be proved true or false, and a statement of *opinion* expresses ideas or feelings. Invite students to list facts they read about New York, Paris, and the Statue of Liberty in this book. Then ask them to list any opinions they might find in the book. Suggest that as they read, students can add more facts and opinions to their list.

QUESTIONING Tell students that good readers ask *questions* and find answers while they read. Good questions often start with a *who, what, when, where, why,* or *how*. Ask students to write down questions they have while reading about the Statue of Liberty.

ADDITIONAL SKILL INSTRUCTION

MAIN IDEA Tell students that the *main idea* is the most important idea about the topic. Have students determine the main idea of this book. Ask: What is this book about in a few words? (the Statue of Liberty) What is the most important idea about this topic? (The statue was offered as a symbol of friendship and took several years to complete.)

Fact and Opinion

- A statement of **fact** is a statement that can be proved true or false. You can check a statement of fact by looking in reference sources, asking an expert, or observing.
- A statement of **opinion** is a person's beliefs or ideas about something. You cannot prove whether it is true or false.

Directions Decide whether each sentence below is a statement of fact or opinion. Write your answer on the line.

1. The Statue of Liberty was a gift from the people of France to honor the friendship between France and America.

_____

2. In 1883, Frederic Auguste Bartholdi made models of every part of the statue, including the crown and tablet, before building it.

_____

3. One of the most amazing sights you can see in New York is the Brooklyn Bridge.

_____

4. Free band concerts were preformed in Central Park during the summers in the 1880s.

_____

5. Thousand of New Yorkers thought the sight of the Statue of Liberty being unveiled was unforgettable.

_____

Name _____

Vocabulary

Directions Fill in the missing letters for each vocabulary word. Then use the word in a sentence.

> ## Check the Words You Know
>
> ___crown   ___liberty   ___models   ___symbol
> ___tablet   ___torch   ___unforgettable   ___unveiled

1. __r__wn _____

_____

2. __ __b__ __ty _____

_____

3. t__ __ch _____

_____

4. __ __for__et__able _____

_____

5. m__de__s _____

_____

6. __ __mbol _____

_____

7. t__ __let _____

_____

8. un__ei__ed _____

_____

New York's Chinatown

SUMMARY This book describes New York City's Chinatown. It describes the people who live there, as well as the sights, sounds, and traditions of this colorful and lively neighborhood. It discusses several important celebrations, like the Chinese New Year. It even gives a recipe for moon cakes.

LESSON VOCABULARY

bows	chilly	foolish
foreign	narrow	perches
recipe		

INTRODUCE THE BOOK

INTRODUCE THE TITLE AND AUTHOR Introduce students to the title and the author of the book *New York's Chinatown*. Ask students what they think this book will be about, based on the title. Does the cover of the book offer any clues? Can they imagine what some of the sights and sounds of Chinatown might be?

BUILD BACKGROUND Discuss with students what they know about Chinatown. Ask them whether they have ever visited Chinatown in New York or another city. What do they remember about their visit? What surprised them the most? What are their favorite types of Chinese food? Have they ever eaten with chopsticks?

PREVIEW/USE PHOTOS AND CAPTIONS Invite students to look through the photographs, charts, and captions in the book. Ask students what they think the text could be about now that they have taken a look at the photographs and read the captions.

ELL Ask if any students have ever been to a Chinatown, whether in New York or elsewhere. Have them describe one thing they remember seeing or hearing while there. If you have any students from China, have them describe what they enjoy about Chinese New Year or discuss another custom, such as eating with chopsticks.

READ THE BOOK

SET PURPOSE Most students will be interested in reading this book so that they can learn about Chinatown, a special neighborhood in New York City. Remind students that interest in other cultures is an important attitude to have.

STRATEGY SUPPORT: INFERRING Tell students to keep in mind what they already know about Chinatown while they read. Ask them to apply this knowledge to the story.

COMPREHENSION QUESTIONS

PAGE 5 Are the streets of Chinatown wide and straight? *(No, they are short, winding, and narrow.)*

PAGE 7 What languages do you think you might hear walking through Chinatown? *(Chinese and English)*

PAGE 8 Why do many Chinese people like to practice the art of Tai Chi? *(to exercise their minds and bodies)*

PAGE 12 Does the Chinese New Year happen on the same date as traditional American New Year? *(No, it happens sometime in January or February.)*

REVISIT THE BOOK

READER RESPONSE

1. Streets are crowded and busy; important Chinese traditions are falling away; there are many choices of food and other products.
2. Responses will vary but should be based on the topic of New York's Chinatown.
3. chilly, narrow, crowded, loud, noisy, colorful
4. Answers will vary but may include speaking politely and listening when someone is speaking to you.

EXTEND UNDERSTANDING Ask students: Why did the photographs help you picture Chinatown much more clearly than if they were illustrations? What is it about a photograph that makes you feel like you are right there in the middle of the action?

RESPONSE OPTIONS

WRITING Have students imagine that they are attending the New Year's parade in Chinatown. Have them describe the sights, sounds, and smells. Describe the noises of the firecrackers and the fireworks. What kinds of music do they hear? What kinds of people line the streets to watch the parade? Have students write about how it feels to be at the parade.

SOCIAL STUDIES CONNECTION

Time For SOCIAL STUDIES

Have students research Chinese immigration on the Internet or in the library. What were the years when the highest numbers of Chinese people came to this country? What cities in the United States did the Chinese tend to immigrate to? What kind of work did Chinese people tend to find once they arrived?

Skill Work

TEACH/REVIEW VOCABULARY

Encourage student pairs to find the vocabulary words in the text. Have them define the words and then work together to write a sentence for each word.

TARGET SKILL AND STRATEGY

CAUSE AND EFFECT Remind students that an *effect* is what happened and a *cause* is why something happened. Have students read page 8. Ask: Name one reason why the older generation feels that their traditions are slipping away. (*Younger Chinese do not bow to their elders.*) Or ask: Name one reason why Chinese people don't celebrate individual birthdays. (*They just add a year each New Year.*)

INFERRING Ask students if using their prior knowledge helped them better understand the story or learn something new. Model inferring by using page 11. Say: I know that people who have moved out of their country and into New York try to keep their culture alive there. I read that the Moon Festival is a Chinese holiday that is celebrated in New York and China. I can infer that the Chinese in New York want to celebrate the Moon Festival there to help keep their traditions alive.

ADDITIONAL SKILL INSTRUCTION

GENERALIZE Remind students that a *generalization* is a broad statement or rule that applies to many examples. Have students compare a traditional American New Year with the Chinese New Year celebration described in the book. What are some of the similarities? (*parades, fireworks, noise, crowds*)

Name _____

Cause and Effect

- A **cause** is *why* something happened.
- An **effect** is *what* happened.

Directions For each cause, write an effect. Use *New York's Chinatown* to help you. The same cause may have different effects.

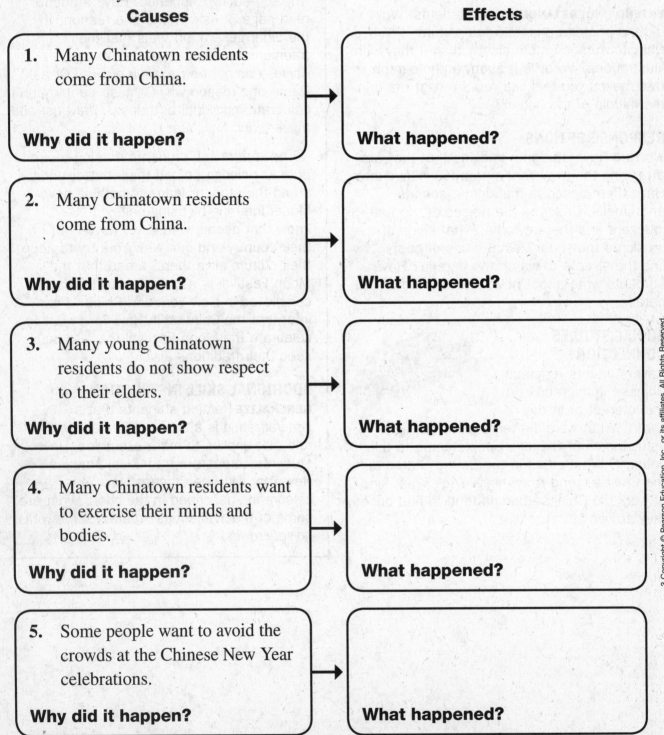

Causes	Effects
1. Many Chinatown residents come from China. **Why did it happen?**	**What happened?**
2. Many Chinatown residents come from China. **Why did it happen?**	**What happened?**
3. Many young Chinatown residents do not show respect to their elders. **Why did it happen?**	**What happened?**
4. Many Chinatown residents want to exercise their minds and bodies. **Why did it happen?**	**What happened?**
5. Some people want to avoid the crowds at the Chinese New Year celebrations. **Why did it happen?**	**What happened?**

Vocabulary

Directions Fill in the blank with the word from the box that matches the definition.

Check the Words You Know

___bows   ___chilly   ___foolish   ___foreign

___narrow   ___perches   ___recipe

1. _____ from a country other than your own

2. _____ places to view things from high above

3. _____ leans forward to show respect

4. _____ silly; not wise

5. _____ instructions for cooking

6. _____ having a small width; not very wide

7. _____ slightly cold

Directions Write a paragraph about Chinatown as described in *New York's Chinatown.* Use at least three vocabulary words.

_____

_____

_____

_____

_____

_____

_____

_____

One Forest, Different Trees

SUMMARY In this story, a girl is encouraged to draw what she feels, instead of conforming to the expectations of her classmates. It supports the lesson concept of freedom of expression in a free society.

LESSON VOCABULARY

encourages   expression
local   native
settled   social
support

INTRODUCE THE BOOK

INTRODUCE THE TITLE AND AUTHOR Discuss with students the title and the author of *One Forest, Different Trees*. Also have students look at the picture on the cover. Explain to students that social studies is the study of how people live as a group. Ask: How might this story have something to do with social studies?

BUILD BACKGROUND Ask students to name their favorite book, and lead them in a short discussion about the differences among the books. Then say: Suppose a law said that everyone had to read the same kind of book. Would that be okay with you? Why or why not?

PREVIEW/USE ILLUSTRATIONS Have students look at the pictures in the book before reading. Ask: Who is the story about? Where does the story happen? Have students read the heading on page 16. Discuss with students whether this page is part of the story.

READ THE BOOK

SET PURPOSE Have students set a purpose for reading *One Forest, Different Trees*. Students may need help setting their own purposes. Ask: Do you want to know why there are so many drawings of trees?

STRATEGY SUPPORT: IMPORTANT IDEAS Remind students that how a story is presented can help them find important ideas. Explain that these ideas will help the students understand why the author wrote the selection. Tell students to look at page 11 and identify the important ideas from each paragraph. Model using page 7. Say: Before I read this page, I knew that an important idea would be about how Sue was sad because of the illustration.

ELL Students may have difficulty with the words *wavy* (page 3), *lollipops* (page 4), and *octopus* and *monkey* (page 11). For each of these terms, draw representative pictures and have students label them in English.

COMPREHENSION QUESTIONS

PAGE 3 How are the children in Sue's class alike? *(They want to know how to draw trees.)*

PAGES 3–7 How do the children try to solve the big problem? *(First Sue offers to help. Then Nat shows how to make lollipop trees.)*

PAGES 10–11 Why do you think Sue wants to draw a tree that looks like an octopus and one that looks like a monkey? *(Possible response: Sue enjoys drawing.)*

PAGE 12 Read what Amy says. Is it a statement of fact or a statement of opinion? Why? *(It is a statement of opinion. Possible response: It can't be proved true or false, because some people might not feel like Amy.)*

REVISIT THE BOOK

READER RESPONSE

1. Responses will vary but should include visualization.
2. Responses will vary but should include main details.
3. grows naturally in a certain place
4. He explained that sometimes kids want to do what is easiest, and sometimes they want to do the same things that other kids do.

EXTEND UNDERSTANDING Ask students to think about the characters in this story. Have them make a Venn diagram to compare and contrast two of the characters. Students should fill in the diagram by writing words that represent the similarities and differences between the two characters.

RESPONSE OPTIONS

WRITING Have students review the background information on page 16. Encourage students to express themselves freely by writing a letter to the editor supporting or opposing Nat's opinion in the story.

SOCIAL STUDIES CONNECTION

Have students look up the First Amendment to the U.S. Constitution. Have them list the freedoms it protects. Lead the class in a discussion of these basic rights.

Skill Work

TEACH/REVIEW VOCABULARY

Discuss this week's lesson vocabulary with students. Reinforce word meaning by asking students to complete sentences for each vocabulary word. For example: *A person who helps is a person who _____.*

TARGET SKILL AND STRATEGY

GRAPHIC SOURCES Remind students that graphic sources are diagrams and charts that help readers understand what they read. Suggest that as students read *One Forest, Different Trees*, they make a story map to write the beginning, middle, and end of the story. Remind students that graphic sources can help them determine the story's plot and big idea.

IMPORTANT IDEAS Explain to students that *important ideas* are the major ideas in a selection. Tell students to look at page 11 and identify the important ideas from each paragraph. Ask: How do these ideas help you understand why the author wrote *One Forest, Different Trees*?

ADDITIONAL SKILL INSTRUCTION

GENERALIZE Remind students that sometimes when you read, you are given ideas about several things or people and you can make a statement about them all together. This might be how they are mostly alike or all alike in some way. After page 7, ask: How are the other children different from Sue? *(They all wanted to draw green lollipops instead of realistic trees.)*

Graphic Sources

- **Graphic sources** present information visually and can help you better understand text.
- Graphic sources include chart, diagrams, maps, and pictures with captions.

Directions To help you understand the sequence of events in *One Forest, Different Trees* fill out this flow chart.

1. What happened **first?**

_____

_____

_____

2. What happened **next?**

_____

_____

_____

3. What happened **next?**

_____

_____

_____

4. What happened **last?**

_____

_____

_____

Vocabulary

Directions Write the word that best completes each sentence.

> ## Check the Words You Know
>
> ___encourages   ___local   ___settled   ___support
> ___expression   ___native   ___social

1. A great painting can be an _____ of joy.

2. I was born and raised in this town. I am a _____.

3. They discussed the problem and _____ it by coming to an agreement.

4. Sue _____ the other kids to draw the trees any way they like.

5. Nat talked to many kids. He is very _____.

6. Sue went to the _____ art supply store to buy markers.

7. Mr. Martinez will _____ you, no matter how you draw a tree.

Directions Use the words *local*, *support*, and *expression* in a short paragraph.

_____

_____

_____

_____

_____

_____

Swimming in a School

SUMMARY Leo is a young fish who is tired of always swimming in a school of fish. One day he discovers a shipwreck and swims off alone to explore it. In the wreck, he encounters several dangerous situations, so he decides to return to the safety of his school.

LESSON VOCABULARY

crystal	disappeared
discovery	goal
journey	joyful
scoop	unaware

INTRODUCE THE BOOK

INTRODUCE THE TITLE AND AUTHOR Discuss with students the title and the author of *Swimming in a School.* Ask students what they think the story might be about, based on the title. Have them look at the illustration on the front cover. Does this picture give them any more clues as to what will happen in the story?

BUILD BACKGROUND Ask students what they know about fish and the ocean. Have them describe any trips they've taken to an aquarium. Have them describe any movies they've seen that have shown fish swimming in schools.

ELL Have students describe a trip to the ocean. Have they ever gone fishing in the ocean? Have they ever been to an aquarium? Have them talk about any of these experiences.

PREVIEW/USE ILLUSTRATIONS Invite students to look at all the illustrations in the book. Ask students how the illustrations give clues as to the meaning of the story.

READ THE BOOK

SET PURPOSE Have students set a purpose for reading *Swimming in a School.* Have them follow the plot closely by taking notes as they read.

STRATEGY SUPPPORT: STORY STRUCTURE Share with students that *story structure* is the way a story is organized and this story tells the events in sequence or in the order in which they happened. Ask students to map out the story's chain of events in a graphic organizer during or after reading

COMPREHENSION QUESTIONS

PAGE 4 What does Leo's friend Gil think about swimming in a school? *(that it's cool)*

PAGE 6 What does Gil say to Leo about the ship? *(that it could be dangerous, that he might get eaten)*

PAGE 9 What is the first danger Leo finds on the ship? *(an anglerfish with its mouth open)*

PAGE 11 What kind of a fish does Leo find lurking in the corner? *(a huge moray eel that wants to eat him)*

PAGE 13 What happens to Leo as he is fleeing the shipwreck? *(A net comes down around him, but he is able to swim through the holes in the net.)*

PAGE 14 Where does Leo go when he just needs a safe place to think? *(behind some coral)*

REVISIT THE BOOK

READER RESPONSE

1. Possible response: Beginning: Leo is bored with always swimming in his school. Middle: Leo swims into an old ship and encounters dangers. End: Leo returns to the safety of his school.
2. Responses will vary but should show understanding of story structure.
3. Responses will vary but should show an understanding and correct usage of words.
4. Possible response: Advantages of doing things in a group include enjoying safety in numbers, getting help when you need it, and learning from each other. Advantages of doing things alone are that you don't have to compromise, and you can do whatever you want.

EXTEND UNDERSTANDING Have students think about what elements of this story make it a fantasy. Have them list details from the story that describe things that could not really happen.

RESPONSE OPTIONS

WRITING Have students imagine that they are a fish swimming in a large school of fish. Rather than going off on their own, like Leo, students should imagine that they stay with the group all day. Ask students: What is it like to swim in a school? What did you see during the day? How does staying in a large group allow you to be safer from larger creatures who might want to eat you?

SCIENCE CONNECTION

Have students research fish schools. Assign each student a different type of fish. They can use the Internet or the library. Have them draw pictures of their fish. Once they have gathered all their information, have them share it with the class.

Skill Work

TEACH/REVIEW VOCABULARY

Encourage student pairs to find the vocabulary words in the text. Have them define the words and then work together to write a sentence for each word.

TARGET SKILL AND STRATEGY

PLOT AND THEME Remind students that the *plot* is the sequence of events that take a story from the beginning to the middle to the end. Also, remind students that stories usually have one big idea or *theme*. Discuss with students what they think the big idea is in a familiar story like *The Tortoise and the Hare* (slow and steady wins the race). Have them tell the plot of the story by recalling the events in sequence.

STORY STRUCTURE Ask students to fill out their graphic organizers as they read, listing chain of events in the story. Remind students that not all events are important and need to be listed. Discuss the important events in the story.

ADDITIONAL SKILL INSTRUCTION

REALISM AND FANTASY Remind students that a *realistic story* tells about something that could happen, while a *fantasy* is a story about something that could not happen. As they read this story, have them think about which elements of the story are realistic and which are fantasy.

Plot and Theme

- The **plot** is an organized pattern of events.
- The **theme** is the "big idea" of a story.

Directions Fill in the graphic organizer about the story elements in *Swimming in School*.

Title _____

This story is about _____

_____
(name the characters)

This story takes place _____

_____
(where and when)

The action begins when _____

_____

Then, _____

_____

Next, _____

_____

After that, _____

_____

The story ends when _____

_____

Theme: _____

_____

Name _____

Vocabulary

Directions Fill in the blank with the word from the box that fits best.

Check the Words You Know

___crystal	___disappeared	___discovery	___goal
___journey	___joyful	___scoop	___unaware

---

1. Leo didn't listen to his friend Gil and set off on his _____.

2. The fisherman tried to _____ the fish out of the water with the net.

3. The flashing _____ caught Leo's eye.

4. Leo was hoping to make an exciting _____ on his adventure.

5. The fish in the school were _____ when Leo returned safely.

6. Leo swam so fast it looked as if he had _____.

7. Leo's _____ was to explore the ship.

8. Leo was _____ of what would happen on his journey.

Directions Write a brief paragraph discussing Leo's journey, using as many vocabulary words as possible.

_____

_____

_____

_____

_____

_____

_____

_____

Greek Myths

SUMMARY This book gives a brief overview of Greek myths, including examples of several gods and goddesses who are characters in many of them.

LESSON VOCABULARY

aqueducts	content
crouched	guidance
honor	pillar
thermal	

INTRODUCE THE BOOK

INTRODUCE THE TITLE AND AUTHOR Discuss the title and author of *Greek Myths.* Point out that the statue in the photograph was made in ancient Greece, thousands of years ago.

BUILD BACKGROUND On a world map, show students the country of Greece. Explain that people who lived there in ancient times are known now for many things in addition to the myths they believed in. One result is that many English words have roots from the ancient Greek language. An example is our word *democracy,* from the Greek word *dēmocratía.* which meant "popular government," or power derived from people.

PREVIEW/USE TEXT FEATURES Ask students to preview the book by paging through it and looking at the illustrations and headings. Draw attention to the glossary on page 16 and invite volunteers to tell how they might use it.

READ THE BOOK

SET PURPOSE Invite students to brainstorm one or more purposes for reading, based on what they found when they previewed the book.

STRATEGY SUPPORT: INFERRING Tell students that good readers often "read between the lines" to figure out what a myth is trying to explain. Students can combine what they read with what they already know to create their own ideas about the story. Then they can go further to infer a lesson or to interpret what they have read.

COMPREHENSION QUESTIONS

PAGES 3 Why did many ancient people make up myths? *(to explain such natural events as thunderstorms before the scientific explanations had been discovered)*

PAGE 6 What does our English word *chaos* mean? *(confusion or complete disorder)* How do you think it is connected to the Greek word Chaos? *(Our word must have come from the Greek word, which referred to the beginning of time where land, sea, and air were all mixed up—in confusion and complete disorder.)*

PAGE 9 What did the Greeks believe made things happen? *(the gods and goddesses)*

PAGES 11–14 Which Greek god established the laws for the island of Atlantis? *(Poseideon)* What do you think was the terrible curse Poseidon told the people of Atlantis they would suffer if they broke his laws? *(That they would no longer exist.)* What makes you think so? *(Because when they did disobey, Zeus got angry and the island and people of Atlantis completely disappeared.)*

REVISIT THE BOOK

READER RESPONSE

1. Generalizations will vary. Supporting facts may include: no scientific explanation yet existed for natural events; Zeus was the mightiest of all; Poseidon governed the sea.
2. Responses will vary, but students may infer that, since Poseidon was the god of the sea, the island and all its people fell to the bottom of the sea.
3. The word *aqueducts* is on page 13. An aqueduct was a series of ducts, or pipes, that carried water from one place to another. Today we have many pipes that carry water from place to place; they are usually underground.
4. Responses may vary, but most students will say that the people of Atlantis should have obeyed the laws of Poseidon.

ELL Students whose native language is Spanish (or one of the other Romance languages such as French, Italian, or Portuguese) should understand that the word meaning "water" is a base for the word *aqueducts*. Note that *aqua* is from the Latin word for water, not from a Greek word.

EXTEND UNDERSTANDING Invite students to tell what they know about myths in general. Point out that most ancient peoples invented myths that explained nature. Explain that because most people at that time could not read or write, the myths were simply told orally by each generation to the next.

RESPONSE OPTIONS

ART/LANGUAGE ARTS Invite students to make up a new myth about one of the gods or goddesses mentioned in the book. Students may illustrate their myth, tell it orally to the class, or write it.

SOCIAL STUDIES CONNECTION

Time For SOCIAL STUDIES

Provide an assortment of myths of all kinds. Ask students to choose one of them, read it, and share with the class what it is about, what it explains, and what part of the world it is from.

Skill Work

TEACH/REVIEW VOCABULARY

Point out to students that the word *content* means "happy with what one has" when it is pronounced with the accent on the second syllable but that it has a different meaning when the accent is put on the first syllable. Pronounce the word both ways for students and challenge them to explain the meaning of the word accented on the first syllable. Then ask them to use each in an oral sentence.

TARGET SKILL AND STRATEGY

GENERALIZE Recall with students that a broad statement that covers many different examples is a *generalization*. Provide several examples, such as *Most of you like to play on the swings* or *Many of you are good at catching balls*. Remind students that generalizations must be supported by observable facts or statements. Both generalizations above might be supported by personal observations.

INFERRING Remind students that they can put together what they already know with what they read to make a decision about something. Tell students they practiced inferring when they figured out what must have happened to Atlantis.

ADDITIONAL SKILL INSTRUCTION

AUTHOR'S PURPOSE Discuss with students that authors usually have their readers in mind when they write something. The authors have a purpose for writing. For example, an author may write a story to entertain readers. Discuss what the author's purpose for writing *Greek Myths* might be.

Generalize

- A **generalization** is a broad statement that applies to many examples.

Directions Choose one of the generalizations about the book *Greek Myths* listed below. Write the generalization in the top box. Then find three statements from the book that support that generalization. Write the statements in the boxes.

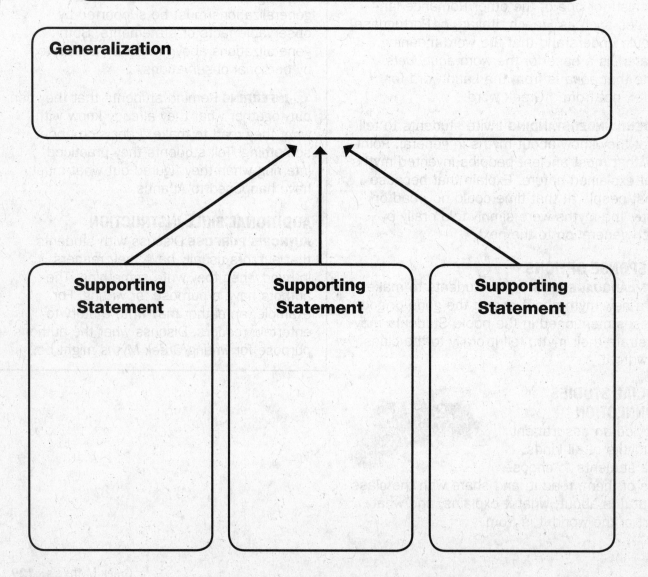

Possible Generalizations

Ancient people made up stories called myths to explain natural events.

Some ancient myths were about gods and goddesses.

Greek gods and goddesses each ruled over one part of life.

Generalization

Supporting Statement

Supporting Statement

Supporting Statement

Name _____

Vocabulary

Directions Write the vocabulary word that fits in each sentence.

Check the Words You Know

___aqueducts	___content	___crouched	___guidance
___honor	___pillar	___thermal	

---

1. Put the plant by the _____ at the edge of the porch.

2. You can still see some ancient Roman _____ in Europe.

3. Mom _____ down to fix the baby's hat.

4. Dad gave me some _____ when I learned to pitch.

5. At first the people were _____ with Poseidon's rules.

6. Warm water was piped in to the _____ baths.

7. Our school received a special _____ for recycling.

Directions Choose three of the vocabulary words. Write a sentence of your own that includes each one.

8. _____

9. _____

10. _____

Story Prediction from Previewing

Title _____

Read the title and look at the pictures in the story.
What do you think a problem in the story might be?

I think a problem might be _____

_____

_____

After reading _____,
draw a picture of one of the problems in the story.

Story Prediction from Vocabulary

Title and Vocabulary Words

Read the title and the vocabulary words.
What do you think this story might be about?

I think this story might be about _____

_____

_____

After reading _____ ,
draw a picture that shows what the story is about.

KWL Chart

Topic _____

What We **K**now	What We **W**ant to Know	What We **L**earned

Vocabulary Frame

Word

Association or Symbol

Predicted definition: _____

_____

One good sentence:

_____

_____

_____

Verified definition: _____

_____

_____

Another good sentence:

_____

_____

_____

Story Predictions Chart

Title _____

What might happen?	What clues do I have?	What did happen?

Story Sequence A

Title _____

Beginning

↓

Middle

↓

End

Story Sequence B

Title	
Characters	**Setting**

Events
1. First

2. Next

3. Then

4. Last

Story Sequence C

Title

Characters

Problem

Events

_____

_____

_____

_____

_____

_____

_____

Solution

Question the Author

Title _____

Author _____ **Page** _____

1. What does the author tell you?	
2. Why do you think the author tells you that?	
3. Does the author say it clearly?	
4. What would make it clearer?	
5. How would you say it instead?	

Story Comparison

Title A _____

_____

Characters

Setting

Events

Title B _____

_____

Characters

Setting

Events

Web

Main Idea

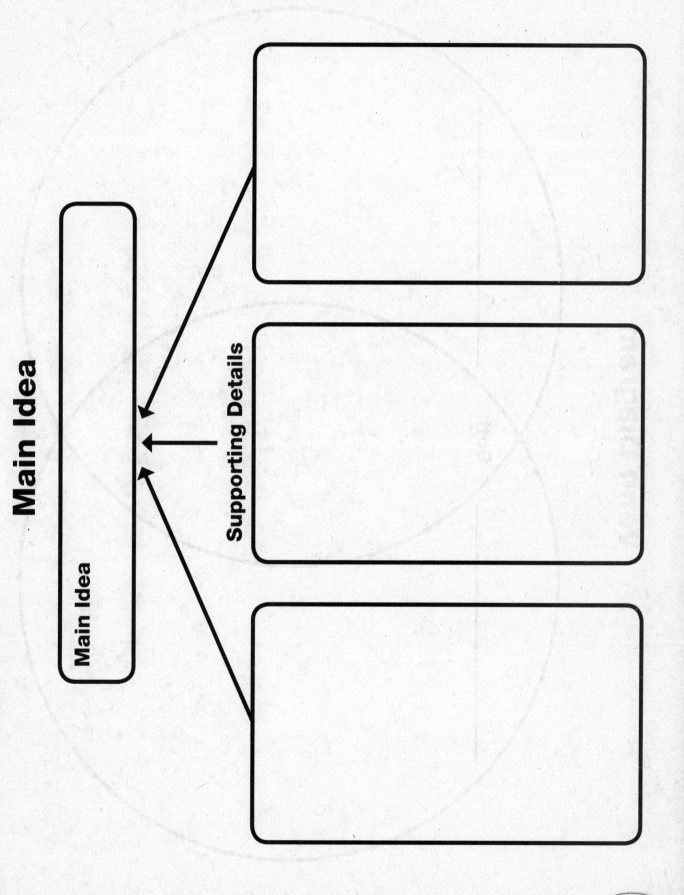

Main Idea

Supporting Details

Venn Diagram

Both

Compare and Contrast

Topics

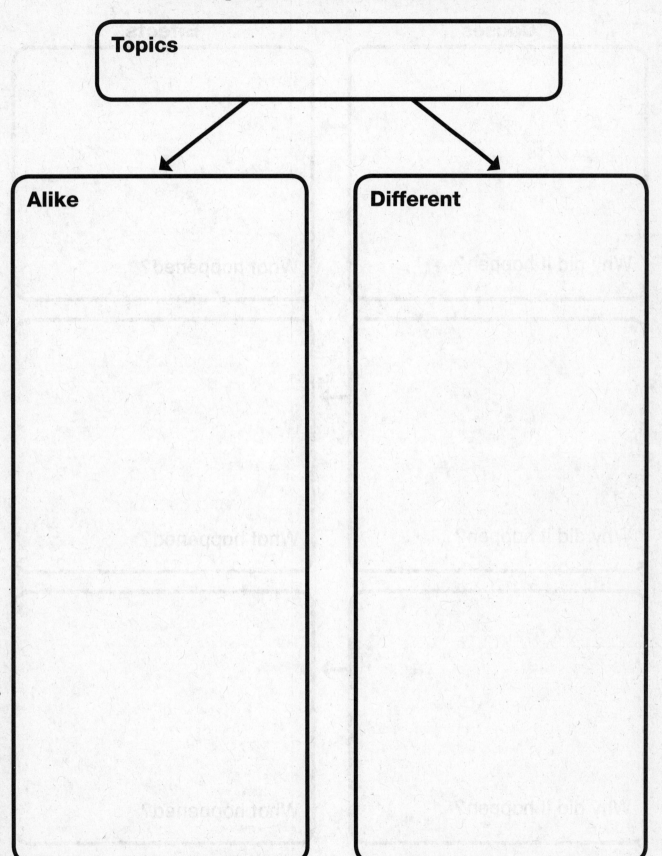

Alike

Different

Cause and Effect

Causes   **Effects**

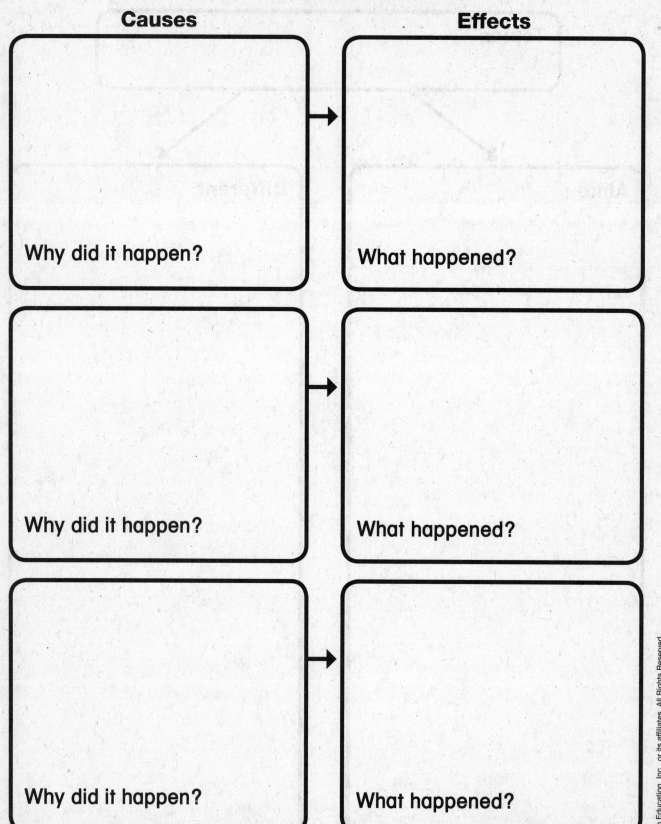

Why did it happen?   What happened?

Why did it happen?   What happened?

Why did it happen?   What happened?

Problem and Solution

Problem

Attempts to Solve the Problem

Solution

Time Line

Date _____

Steps in a Process

Process _____

Step 1

↓

Step 2

↓

Step 3

Three-Column Chart

Four-Column Chart

Four-Column Graph

Title _____

Answer Key

Leveled Reader Practice Pages

The Opposite Cousins p. 14

⟐ **CHARACTER AND SETTING**

Characters: Samantha—likes to swim in the lake, likes to fish, eager to teach Jeff how to fish, plays computer games with Jeff; Jeff—upset when his computer does not work, plays on his computer, goes fishing with Samantha, wants to create a computer fishing game. Setting: in the country near a lake; a cabin Paragraphs will vary but should reflect an understanding that Samantha and Jeff have different interests but eventually find they have things in common.

The Opposite Cousins p. 15 Vocabulary
1. fuel
2. bat
3. battery
4. plug
5. blew
6. term
7. vision
8–10. Sentences will vary but should demonstrate correct meanings.

It's A Fair Swap! p. 18

⟐ **SEQUENCE**
1. People had no money but needed goods.
2. Native Americans bartered with Europeans for furs and skins and received things they couldn't make with their own tools; colonist traded with each other.
3. As the country grew, people began to use money to buy goods from local merchants.
4. Money was used far more often than bartering. Bartering still survives today. Goods and services are traded on the Internet.

It's A Fair Swap! p. 19 Vocabulary
1. carpenter
2. knowledge
3. marketplace
4. plenty
5. straying
6. thread
7. carpetmaker
8. merchant
9. carpenter
10. thread

11. straying
12. plenty
13. merchant or marketplace
14. knowledge
15. carpetmaker
16. marketplace or merchant
17–18. Sentences will vary but should show an understanding of the vocabulary words.

Life in the Arctic p. 22

⟐ **SEQUENCE**

Possible responses:
1. The Inuit, like many other ancient people, invented or developed new technology to help make life easier.
2. At first, early Inuit hunters used small sleds, pulled by the hunters themselves, to transport game after a hunt.
3. Then, as the Inuit were able to domesticate dogs, they developed the dog sled.
4. As technology developed even further, the Inuit began to rely on snowmobiles.

Life in the Arctic p. 23 Vocabulary
1. d
2. a
3. e
4. f
5. b
6. c

Paragraphs will vary but should demonstrate students' understanding of the vocabulary.

Let's Surprise Mom p. 26

⟐ **COMPARE AND CONTRAST**

Responses will vary but should show understanding of comparing and contrasting.

Let's Surprise Mom p. 27 Vocabulary
1. thousands—multiples of ten hundred; a very large number of things
2. section—a separate part or division
3. spoiled—damaged or unfit to use
4. laundry—clothes washed or to be washed
5. traded
6. variety
7. shelves
8. store

E-mail Friends p. 30
AUTHOR'S PURPOSE
1–2. To inform and to entertain
3. To show the similarities (working with wildlife) and differences (working with zebras or grizzly bears) between the two jobs.
4. To show the difference of terms used in the two countries

E-mail Friends p. 31 Vocabulary
1. ARRANGED put in a specific order
2. WOBBLED moved unsteadily from side to side
3. ERRANDS short trips taken to do something
4. EXCITEDLY with high emotions
5. STEADY firm in position or place
6. DANGEROUSLY hazardously
7. BUNDLES groups of objects tied together
8. UNWRAPPED removed the outer covering of something
9. Sentences will vary but should show an understanding of the vocabulary words.

The Frozen Continent: Antarctica p. 34
MAIN IDEA AND DETAILS
Possible responses:
1. Antarctica is very windy and dry.
2. Scientists call Antarctica a desert.
3. The small amount of snow that falls in the Antarctica never melts.
4. Snow is moved around by the wind until it freezes into ice.

The Frozen Continent: Antarctica p. 35
Vocabulary
1. d
2. e
3. f
4. c
5. a
6. g
7. b
8. frozen
9. flippers
10. pecks
11. hatch
Paragraphs will vary but should demonstrate students' understanding of the vocabulary.

Buddy Goes to School p. 38
COMPARE AND CONTRAST
Possible responses:
1. adopted from a shelter
2. graduated with honors
3. mature
4. doesn't snuggle
5. Paragraphs will vary but should be supported with details from the story.

Buddy Goes to School p. 39 Vocabulary
1. mature
2. mention
3. adorable
4. iguana
5. trophies
6. exactly
7. compassionate
8. iguana
9. adorable
10. trophies
11. compassionate
12. mature

The Metal Detective p. 42
DRAW CONCLUSIONS
Possible response:
Facts: Metal detectors beep when they pass over metal. Metal detectors are used on beaches and in parks.
Conclusion: Metal detectors help locate lost things and metals.

The Metal Detective p. 43 Vocabulary
1. c
2. e
3. b
4. a
5. f
6. d
7. enormous
8. strain
9. scattered
10. collection

Growing Vegetables p. 46
AUTHOR'S PURPOSE
Possible responses:
1. to show that when you don't water plants, they wilt
2. to tell about the different things you need to do to grow vegetables
3. to inform the reader how to grow a vegetable garden
4. They need water, weeding, and sunlight.
5. It's more fun for everyone, and the end result is better.

Growing Vegetables p. 47 Vocabulary

1. b
2. c
3. b
4. a
5. c
6. b
7. a
8. cheated
9. clever
10. bottom
11. crops
12. partners
13. lazy
14. wealth

All About Birds p. 50

MAIN IDEA AND DETAILS

1. All birds are similar but also are very different from each other.

Possible responses:

2–4. Some birds eat meat others eat fruit; Birds range in size from the bee humming-bird to the 300–pound ostrich; Birds nests can be small baskets or large platforms.

All About Birds p. 51 Vocabulary

1. platform
2. hunters
3. bill
4. Ton
5. materials, goo
6. Twigs

Sentences will vary but should show an understanding of the vocabulary words.

Raisins p. 54

DRAW CONCLUSIONS

Possible responses:

Fact: The state of California is the only place in our country that produces raisins.

What I Know: Australia is much farther away than California.

Conclusion: The raisins we eat in this country come from California.

Fact: Grapes were given as prizes in some ancient sports events.

What I Know: Prizes are usually something people value highly.

Conclusion: In those ancient times, people thought raisins were a very special treat.

Raisins p. 55 Vocabulary

1. preservative
2. proof
3. raise
4. raisin
5. area
6. artificial
7. grapevine

Sentences will vary but should show an understanding of the vocabulary words.

The Hunters and the Elk p. 58

CHARACTER, PLOT, AND SETTING

1. *The Hunters and the Elk*
2. The Snohomish people, the Creator, the hunters, and the elk
3. Washington State, hundreds of years ago
4. The elk gave the Snohomish people food, clothing, weapons, and art; The Creator gave his leftover languages to the Snohomish people.
5. The Creator did not make the sky high enough; The people pushed the sky higher.
6. Three elk and four hunters were trapped in the sky; The Snohomish people work together to do great things.
7. When people work together they can do great things.
8. The Snohomish people could communicate with one another; The sky would be higher.

The Hunters and the Elk p. 59 Vocabulary

Sentences will vary for 2, 4, 6, and 8 but should show students' understanding of the meaning of the words and correct usage.

1. a
3. b
5. a
7. a

Pictures in the Sky p. 62

GRAPHIC SOURCES

Possible responses:

Big and Little Dipper: same shape, use the Polaris, Big Dipper helps tell direction

Polaris: Helps tell direction, shines brightly, also called the North Star.

Pictures in the Sky p. 63 Vocabulary

1. gigantic
2. dim
3. gases
4. temperature
5. ladle
6. shine
7. patterns

8–11. Sentences will vary but should show an understanding of the vocabulary words.

Rescuing Whales p. 66

⊙ **GENERALIZE**

Possible responses:

Generalization: There are many things to do to help a stranded whale.

Details: pour water and ice on a beached whale; scientists use supplies to do medical tests; herd the whales into a group and push them into deeper water.

Rescuing Whales p. 67 Vocabulary

1. chipped
2. bay
3. melodies
4. channel
5. surrounded
6. anxiously
7. blizzard
8. supplies
9. symphonies

The Field Trip p. 70

⊙ **CAUSE AND EFFECT**

1. e
2. g
3. h
4. a
5. f
6. b
7. c
8. d

The Field Trip p. 71 Vocabulary

1. topic
2. lofty
3. string
4. incredible
5. noble
6. unseen
7. waterless
8. search
9. survivors

The Winning Point! p. 74

⊙ **GENERALIZE**

Generalization: Soccer is similar to basketball.

Possible responses: Two teams of players face each other; they try to get the ball into a goal at the other end of the playing field; They also try to prevent the other team from getting the ball into their goal; The team with the most points wins.

The Winning Point! p. 75 Vocabulary

1. popular
2. terrible
3. basketball
4. disease
5. sports
6. study
7. guard
8. freeze

How to Measure the Weather p. 78

⊙ **GRAPHIC SOURCES**

1. San Antonio, TX
2. Helena, MT
3. Chicago has less snow than Helena and more snow than Boise.
4. It is in a warm climate
5. It is in a cold climate

How to Measure the Weather p. 79 Vocabulary

1. b
2. e
3. f
4. a
5. d
6. h
7. g
8. c

Paragraphs will vary but should include the five vocabulary words used correctly.

Grandpa's Rock Kit p. 82

⊙ **FACT AND OPINON**

1. F
2. F
3. F
4. O
5. F
6. F
7. O
8. F

9–10. Opinion. This statement contains a feeling or belief.

Grandpa's Rock Kit p. 83 Vocabulary

1. chores
2. labeled
3. attic
4. stamps
5. board
6. spare
7. customers

Responses will vary but should show an understanding of the vocabulary words and should clearly be real or imaginary.

Across the English Channel p. 86

⊙ **FACT AND OPINON**

1. fact
2. fact
3. opinion
4. fact
5. opinion

Across the English Channel p. 87 Vocabulary

1. current
2. medal
3. continued
3. drowned
4. stirred
5. continued
6. drowned
7. stirred
8. strokes

Paragraphs will vary but should describe an achievement and correctly use the word celebrate.

Swimming Like Buck p. 90

⊙ **CAUSE AND EFFECT**

a. Other ducks teased Buck.
b. Buck flopped over while trying to swim like the other ducks.
c. The coach told Buck he was a beautiful swimmer.
d. Buck won every race and became famous.
e. Buck was famous, won every race, and was signing autographs.

Swimming Like Buck p. 91 Vocabulary
1. held tightly
2. repeated, as a sound
3. a long, narrow ditch
4. tall plants that grow in ponds
5. rushed or struggled
6. area of land between mountains
7. a small area or patch
8–10. Sentences will vary but should show students' understanding of the vocabulary.

A Tea Party with Obâchan p. 94
🔘 COMPARE AND CONTRAST
Possible responses:
1–2. curious, happy, young
3–4. quiet, loving, caring.
5–6. graceful, knowledgeable, caring, wise
7–8. Responses will vary but should show understanding of comparing and contrasting.

A Tea Party with Obâchan p. 95 Vocabulary
Poems and definitions will vary but should show students' understanding of vocabulary.

Celebrate Independence Day, Celebrar el Día de la Independencia p. 98
🔘 MAIN IDEA AND DETAILS
1. b
2. c
3. a
4–5. Responses will vary but should support the main idea.

Celebrate Independence Day, Celebrar el Día de la Independencia p. 99 Vocabulary
1. difficult   5. piers
2. soar   6. swallow
3. bouquets   7. nibble
4. circus
Paragraphs will vary but should show students' understanding of vocabulary.

A Child's Life in Korea p. 102
🔘 SEQUENCE
1. d   4. b
2. c   5. a
3. e

A Child's Life in Korea p. 103 Vocabulary
1. sick   6. farewell
2. well   7. memories
3. drops   8. Curious
4. port   9. delicious
5. described   10. homesick

The World of Bread! p. 106
🔘 DRAW CONCLUSIONS
Possible response: The dough is shaped in a circle and browned in a fraying pan. + It is held over an open flame, which causes the bread to puff up. → This bread has big air pockets in it.

The World of Bread! p. 107 Vocabulary
1. braided   5. batch
2. mixture   6. bakery
3. boils   7. dough
4. ingredients
Paragraphs will vary but should show students' understanding of vocabulary.

A Walk Around the City p. 110
🔘 AUTHOR'S PURPOSE
Possible responses:
1. to inform about the different jobs in cities
2. to get me to take a walk around my city
3. to get me to think about what my city looks like
4. to show the different types of jobs in a city

A Walk Around the City p. 111 Vocabulary
1. pitcher   5. treasure
2. cardboard   6. ruined
3. feast   7. flights
4. fierce
Paragraphs will vary but should show students' understanding of vocabulary.

The Statue of Liberty: A Gift from France p. 114
🔘 FACT AND OPINION
1. Fact   4. Fact
2. Fact   5. Opinion
3. Opinion

The Statue of Liberty: A Gift from France p. 115 Vocabulary
1. crown   5. models
2. liberty   6. symbol
3. torch   7. tablet
4. unforgettable   8. unveiled
Sentences will vary but should show students' understanding of vocabulary.

New York's Chinatown p. 118
CAUSE AND EFFECT
Possible responses:
1. Throughout Chinatown, you can hear people speaking Chinese.
2. Many Chinese traditions are maintained in Chinatown.
3. Some older residents of Chinatown are disappointed in the younger generation.
4. Some Chinatown residents practice Tai Chi.
5. Some people watch the celebrations from perches above the city streets.

New York's Chinatown p. 119 Vocabulary
1. foreign
2. perches
3. bows
4. foolish
5. recipe
6. narrow
7. chilly

Paragraphs will vary but should show students' understanding of vocabulary.

One Forest, Different Trees p. 122
GRAPHIC SOURCES
Possible responses:
1. First, the class decided to make a big picture for the wall.
2. Next, Sue was sad because everyone drew trees that looked like green lollipops.
3. Mr. Martinez explained that drawing a tree that looks like a lollipop might be easier for some kids.
4. Everyone learned to appreciate different types of drawings.

One Forest, Different Trees p. 123 Vocabulary
1. expression
2. settled
3. settled
4. encourages
5. social
6. local
7. support

Paragraphs will vary but should show students' understanding of vocabulary.

Swimming in a School p. 126
PLOT AND THEME
Title: *Swimming in a School*; a fish named Leo; under the sea; Leo swims away from the school to look at a ship; Leo confronts an angler fish; he confronts a moray eel; he gets caught in a net but is able to swim through it; he rejoins the school. It's best to stick with the group.

Swimming in a School p. 127 Vocabulary
1. journey
2. scoop
3. crystal
4. discovery
5. joyful
6. disappeared
7. goal
8. unaware

Paragraphs will vary but should include the five vocabulary words used correctly.

Greek Myths p. 130
GENERALIZE
Possible response:
Generalization: Ancient people made up stories called myths to explain natural events.
Supporting Statements: Ancient people wanted to understand natural events but did not have the scientific knowledge that explained them; In ancient Greece, myths were about gods and goddesses who ruled the world and everything in it; The Greeks made up myths to tell what might happen if people disobeyed laws.

Greek Myths p. 131 Vocabulary
1. pillar
2. aqueducts
3. crouched
4. guidance
5. content
6. thermal
7. honor
8–10. Responses will vary but should show students' understanding of vocabulary.